S0-AVX-081

Cooking with Five Ingredients or Less

Cooking with Five Ingredients or Less

Susan Kosoff and Teresa Kennedy

McGRAW-HILL BOOK COMPANY

New York   St. Louis   San Francisco
Hamburg   Mexico   Toronto

Copyright © 1984 by Susan Kosoff and Teresa
Kennedy. All rights reserved. Printed in the United
States of America. Except as permitted under the
Copyright Act of 1976, no part of this publication may
be reproduced or distributed in any form or by any
means or stored in a data base or retrieval system,
without the prior written permission of the publisher.

1 2 3 4 5 6 7 8 9 FGRFGR 8 7 6 5 4

ISBN 0-07-035479-0{PBK.}
ISBN 0-07-035288-7{HC}

LIBRARY OF CONGRESS CATALOGING IN PUBLICATION DATA

Kosoff, Susan
Cooking with five ingredients or less.
1. Cookery,   I. Kennedy, Teresa. II. Title.
III. Title: Cooking with 5 ingredients or less.
TX652.K58 1984   641.5   83-22279

ISBN 0-07-035479-0{PBK.}
ISBN 0-07-035288-7{HC}

Book design by Iris Weinstein

Illustrations by Laura Hartman

Special thanks to Andy, Paul, and Ginny, who encouraged us the most, and to Ruby, Grace, and Rusty, who ate what nobody else would.

Contents

∽ Introduction ∾

According to an old joke, there are two kinds of people in the world—those who divide the world into two kinds of people and those who don't. When it comes to cooking, we belong to the first category. In our experience, cooks generally fall into two categories: those who cook because they want to and those who cook because they have to.

Eating is another story. Everybody eats, and almost without exception the better the food, the happier we are. And so that becomes the primary aim of this book— to give cooks of either persuasion a collection of ways to prepare really good food. Whether you find cooking an art or a chore, this book is for you. In collecting and developing these recipes, we hope to celebrate the art and, at the same time, remove the drudgery. We don't believe that delicious food should be available only to a select few. We hope, instead, to make beautiful food accessible to every kind of cook, and to everyone who eats.

Why five ingredients? Because we found ourselves searching for easy recipes that don't require special ingredients, shopping trips, or long hours in the kitchen. What we wanted were great meals, whether or not we wanted to cook.

For example, how many times have you come home, tired and hungry, to a refrigerator containing nothing but a chicken, a jar of mustard, and half a bottle of honey? Any good cook will tell you to use what you have on hand, and that is the heart of this book: to include recipes composed of foods generally found in the cupboard. Our recipes don't require exotic, hard-to-find ingredients, a lot of time, or even a lot of expertise. We would hope that our collection is diverse enough and easy enough to break the sandwich habit, or the "if it's Tuesday, it must be frankfurters" blues.

And the reverse is true, too. How many times have you come home to nothing at all in your refrigerator? With these recipes, you know exactly what you need to get at the grocery store, and you don't have to spend half your salary or half your day shopping for ingredients.

There is nothing magical about five ingredients, except that the majority of recipes found in cookbooks and periodicals tend to be too costly, too complicated, or too time-consuming for the way we cook today.

We have tried to include a collection with as much variety as possibly. "Cooking for One or Two" takes into account the smaller household, and at the back of each chapter we have included an "Easy Exotics" section for those times when you are looking for something a little different. You will find recipes here that are equally appropriate for a simple Sunday night supper or a once-a-year elegant dinner party. In fact, with some of our special entrées, you may find that you can treat yourself and your family to a special meal more often than you thought possible.

Five-ingredient cooking has some other advantages as well. Many of our recipes are low in salt, and very few contain prepackaged ingredients. In this way, you can avoid the preservatives, additives, and additional expense of many so-called "convenience foods."

Each recipe is complete in and of itself. We have allowed ourselves a little latitude (we don't count water as an ingredient, for example), and occasionally we have included an optional ingredient. If you like, you may choose to include additional seasonings or garnishes with these recipes, and the results will still be successful.

Be creative if you wish, let the recipes stand if you prefer. Either way, either kind of cook wins, and so will family, friends, and all of the rest of us who love to eat.

Appetizers
and
Soups

Appetizers and first courses are important to any meal because of their primary purpose—to whet the appetite for things to come. When serving appetizers with dinner, try never to overdo it. Your guests will be too full to really appreciate the effort that has gone into the rest of the meal. For cocktail parties and the like, however, feel free to include as much variety and flavor as you can possibly come up with. Not only will your guests be grateful for enough to eat, but the rich, spicy quality of hors d'oeuvres and appetizers will do much to counteract the effects of too much liquid refreshment.

ANCHOVY DIP

2   2-ounce cans anchovy
     fillets, drained
3   tablespoons red wine
     vinegar
1/2 cup olive oil
4   cloves garlic, crushed
1/4 cup chopped fresh
     parsley

Combine all ingredients in work bowl of blender or food processor and process until smooth. Transfer to serving dish. Chill at least 2 hours before serving. Use as a dip for crackers or fresh crudités. **Makes 1¼ cups.**

APRICOT RUMAKI

An interesting variation on an old favorite.

    Boiling water
12 slices bacon
24 dried apricot halves

Preheat oven to 375° F. Place bacon in dish and pour boiling water over to cover. Let stand 5 minutes; drain and dry bacon. Stretch bacon as long as possible; cut each slice in half. Wrap each half around an apricot and secure with a toothpick. Bake until bacon has cooked. Serve hot. **Makes 24.**

BABY BEEF WELLINGTON APPETIZER

This can be made ahead and stored in the refrigerator until serving time. Reheat in a 350° F oven 15 minutes before serving.

1½ **pounds thick sirloin steak, cut into 2-inch cubes**
1 **4-ounce can goose liver pâté**
1 **17½-ounce package frozen puff pastry, defrosted**
1 **egg white, beaten**

Preheat oven to 350° F. Spread each beef cube with ½ teaspoon pâté. Cut pastry sheets into 3-inch squares. Place a beef cube in the center of each pastry square and fold up sides. Moisten edges with a little bit of water to seal securely. Transfer to ungreased baking sheet, seam side down. Brush with beaten egg white and pierce top of pastry with a fork. Bake until puffed and golden, about 35 minutes. **Makes 15 to 20.**

BLUE CHEESE APPETIZER

6 ounces blue cheese, crumbled
¾ cup butter
½ teaspoon white pepper
¼ cup ground pistachio nuts

Combine cheese, butter, and pepper in work bowl of blender or food processor and process until light and smooth. Form into a ball and roll in ground pistachio nuts. Serve with crackers or toast rounds. This will keep up to 2 weeks in refrigerator if well covered.

EVER-READY CHEESE

4 cups shredded cheese (the more variety, the better)
3 ounces cream cheese, softened
2 tablespoons olive oil
2 teaspoons dry mustard
3 tablespoons sherry

Puree all ingredients in work bowl of food processor or blender. Pack into a container, cover and refrigerate at least a week before using. Any odds and ends of cheese can be blended and added to the crock while cheese is soft. Replenish oil, mustard, and wine as needed.

CHEESE COOKIES

$^2/_3$ **cup butter, at room temperature**
$^3/_4$ **cup shredded cheddar cheese, at room temperature**
2   **egg yolks**
$^1/_2$ **teaspoon sugar**
1$^3/_4$ **cup all-purpose flour, sifted**

Preheat oven to 350° F. In a medium bowl, beat butter and cheese until smooth; add egg yolks and blend well. Beat in sugar. Add flour to form a stiff dough. Put dough through a cookie press. Place cookies 1 inch apart on a greased baking sheet; bake 12 minutes, or until lightly browned. If preferred, the dough can be chilled, rolled out, and cut with cookie cutters. **Makes 3 dozen.**

CHILI CHEESE DIP

Hot and spicy—but not too much so.

1   **4-ounce can green chili peppers**
1   **cup sour cream**
$^1/_2$ **cup finely chopped onion**
1   **8-ounce package cream cheese, softened**
Light cream

Put chili peppers, sour cream, onion, and cream cheese in work bowl of blender or food processor and process until smooth, adding cream as necessary to achieve desired consistency. **Makes about 2 cups.**

CHICKEN LIVERS MARSALA

A really elegant first course. If preferred, serve the chicken livers as a main course, omitting toast triangles and substituting ½ cup cooked rice per serving.

4 **slices lean bacon, diced**

2 **pounds chicken livers, cut in half**

1 **teaspoon dried sage or rosemary**

½ **cup Marsala wine**

18 **toast triangles**

Place bacon in a heavy skillet and sauté 1 minute. Add liver and sage and cook over medium heat 3 to 4 minutes. Liver should be pink on the inside. Transfer to a warm plate. Add wine to skillet, scraping up bits of liver and bacon with a wooden spoon. Simmer sauce 2 minutes over medium heat to thicken slightly. Arrange livers on toast; spoon sauce over. Serve immediately. **Makes about 18 toast triangles, or serves 4 as a main course.**

GARLIC-DILL SPREAD

1/2   **cup butter, softened**
1   **clove garlic, crushed**
2   **tablespoons chopped fresh dill**
1/2   **tablespoon chopped fresh parsley**

Combine all ingredients in a small bowl until well blended and spread on crackers or fresh French or Italian bread. **Makes about 1/2 cup.**

STUFFED GOUDA CHEESE

1   **14- to 16-ounce baby Gouda cheese**
1/2   **cup dark beer**
2   **teaspoons Dijon mustard**
1/4   **cup butter**
1   **tablespoon chopped fresh dill**

Cut a large circle in the top of the cheese. Leaving shell intact, hollow out cheese. Cut cheese into smaller chunks, and process with remaining ingredients in work bowl of blender or food processor until smooth. Return cheese mixture to shell. Serve with crackers or pumpernickel bread.

MUSHROOM-CHEESE STRUDEL

Served with a soup and salad, this appetizer becomes a complete meal.

1 **17¹/₂-ounce package frozen puff pastry**
¹/₂ **cup butter**
¹/₂ **pound fresh mushrooms, washed and sliced thin**
1 **egg, beaten**
1¹/₂ **cups shredded sharp cheddar cheese**

Preheat oven to 350° F. Center puff pastry on a tea towel or equivalent cloth, leaving a 2-inch border of cloth on all sides. Allow pastry to thaw 20 minutes. Meanwhile, sauté mushrooms in butter until tender. Cool slightly and add egg and cheese. Mix well. Spread a thin layer of the mushroom mixture along the length of the pastry and, grasping the cloth with both hands gently, lift the pastry and roll up like a jelly roll, being careful to seal the ends. Place the strudel on a cookie sheet, seam side down, and brush with additional butter. Bake for 45 minutes, or until pastry is puffed and golden. Slice and serve hot as an appetizer or hors d'oeuvre. **Serves 8 to 10 as an appetizer, 4 as a main course.**

STUFFED MUSHROOMS

16   large, fresh mushrooms (remove and reserve stems, chopped)

4   tablespoons butter

2   tablespoons Madeira or dry sherry

1/4 to 1/2   cup heavy cream

Grated Parmesan cheese

Preheat oven to 350° F. In a medium saucepan over moderate heat, sauté mushroom stems in butter until liquid has evaporated. Add wine and 1/4 cup cream and cook until liquid has evaporated. Add more cream if desired. Place mushroom caps in a buttered baking dish and stuff the cavities with the filling; top with cheese. Bake about 15 minutes. Place under broiler 1 minute to brown. Serve very hot in the same dish. **Makes 16 mushrooms.**

BAKED MUSSELS

4   pounds mussels, cleaned, beards removed

1   16-ounce can plum tomatoes, drained and chopped

1/4   cup dried bread crumbs

1/4   cup chopped fresh parsley

Olive oil

Preheat oven to 450° F. Place mussels in a large sauce-pan. Add 2 cups water, cover, and steam mussels open. Drain and allow to cool. Remove mussels from shells. Place 2 or 3 mussels in one shell until all mussels have been used. In a small bowl combine tomatoes, bread crumbs, and parsley. Place a small amount over mussels; drizzle with a little oil. Arrange shells in a baking dish and bake about 5 minutes, or until slightly browned. **Makes 15 to 20 shells.**

NACHOS

12 corn tortillas, cut into eighths
   Oil for deep frying
 4 cups shredded mild cheddar cheese
 **1 4-ounce can green chili peppers,
    finely chopped (or substitute 1 4-ounce
    can jalapeño peppers)**

Preheat oven to 400° F. Fry tortillas in 1 inch oil at 375° F a few at a time, stirring to separate. Drain on paper towels. Spread an even layer of tortilla chips in a shallow oven-proof dish. Combine cheese and peppers in a small bowl; then spread evenly over tortilla chips. Bake 15 minutes, or until cheese is melted and bubbly. **Serves 8 to 10.**

POOR MAN'S PÂTÉ

6 slices bacon
1 8-ounce package liverwurst sausage
3 scallions, chopped
2 tablespoons dry sherry
2½ tablespoons butter

Fry bacon until crisp; drain and crumble. Combine bacon, liverwurst, scallions, sherry, and butter in work bowl of food processor or blender and process until smooth. This appetizer is best when made the day before serving and stored in refrigerator. Serve with crackers or toast rounds. **Makes about 1¼ cups.**

POPPY CHEESE STICKS

Dip strips of bread in melted butter, Parmesan cheese, and poppy seeds. Bake at 400° F until browned.

ROJAK (Peanut Dip)

Middle Eastern in origin, this unusual dip is surprisingly good. Use any leftovers to baste chicken or beef strips.

1/3   **cup crunchy peanut butter**

3   **tablespoons brown sugar, firmly packed**

1/2 to 3/4   **teaspoon dried red pepper flakes**

3   **tablespoons tomato-based chili sauce**

1/4   **cup lemon juice**

Thoroughly combine all ingredients. Store at room temperature overnight. Serve as a dip for fresh vegetables. **Makes about 3/4 cup.**

RUBY ROUNDS

1/4   **pound butter, softened**

1   **small (about 1 pound) package party rye bread (small rounds)**

1   **8-ounce jar sauerkraut**

1/2   **pound pastrami, thinly sliced, each slice cut in half**

1/2   **pound Swiss, Gruyère, or Jarlsberg cheese, grated**

Preheat oven to 350° F. Butter bread rounds lightly. Place one slice pastrami and one tablespoon sauerkraut on each round. Top with grated cheese. Place rounds on cookie sheet and bake until cheese bubbles. **Makes about 30 rounds.**

SALAMI TURNOVERS

Everything but the final baking can be done beforehand. Store unbaked turnovers in refrigerator.

- 1 8-ounce can tomato sauce
- 1 cup shredded mozzarella cheese
- 8 ounces hard salami, finely chopped
- 1/2 teaspoon Italian seasoning
- 4 9-inch frozen pie crusts

Preheat oven to 450° F. Mix tomato sauce, mozzarella cheese, salami, and seasoning. Thaw pie crusts about 15 minutes; roll out dough and crimped edges to about 1/8-inch thickness. Cut crusts into approximately 3-inch rounds. Fill the center of each round with about 1 teaspoon filling. Moisten the margin around the filling with a little bit of water before folding and pressing the edges together. Prick the tops of each turnover with a toothpick or skewer to allow steam to escape during baking. Put the turnovers on a baking sheet and place on the middle shelf of the oven. Bake 10 minutes, or until golden brown. Serve hot. **Makes about 25 turnovers.**

SALMON PÂTÉ

Serve as a spread for bagels at your next luncheon or brunch.

1   7³/₄-ounce can salmon
8   ounces cream cheese, softened
¹/₃   cup butter, softened
¹/₄   cup scallion, chopped
1   tablespoon chopped fresh dill

Drain salmon and remove any small bones. Process all
ingredients in work bowl of food processor or blender.
Makes about 1³/₄ cups.

SMOKED TROUT
WITH HORSERADISH-
AND-DILL SAUCE

¹/₂   pound fillet of smoked trout
1   tablespoon horseradish
2   tablespoons chopped fresh dill
¹/₄   cup mayonnaise
¹/₄   cup sour cream

Arrange trout on platter or serving dish. Combine horseradish, dill, mayonnaise, and sour cream until well
blended and serve over fish. **Serves 4.**

EASY

EXOTICS

BABA GHANOUSH

Middle Eastern in origin, this version of eggplant caviar is delicious either as an appetizer, a vegetable course, or a sandwich filling for Middle Eastern pita bread.

1   medium-sized eggplant (about 1 pound)
2   tablespoons tahini (ground sesame-seed paste)
1   large clove garlic, crushed
Juice of ½ lemon (about 2 tablespoons)
Salt to taste

Place eggplant directly on stove burner and roast over very low flame, turning often, or place in 375° oven, until skin has a charred look and eggplant collapses; remove from heat and cool. Scoop out eggplant pulp and transfer to a small bowl. Mash until smooth and combine with remaining ingredients. **Makes about 2 cups.**

BAGNA CAUDA

A must for a classic hot antipasto.

> 2 **cups heavy cream**
> 4 **tablespoons butter**
> 1 **tablespoon chopped garlic**
> 12 **anchovy fillets, chopped**
> **Dash cayenne pepper**

In a small saucepan, reduce cream over moderate heat to approximately 1 cup. Set aside. In a separate pan, melt butter; add anchovies and garlic, and sauté until garlic is golden. Stir in reduced cream and heat. Do not allow to boil. Transfer to a serving dish and add cayenne pepper. Serve hot as a dip. **Makes about 2 cups.**

BORANI

A Middle Eastern spinach spread.

> 1 **medium yellow onion, minced.**
> 1 **clove garlic, crushed**
> 1/4 **cup butter**
> 1¼ **cups chopped cooked spinach,**
> **squeezed to remove excess moisture**
> 1/3 **cup plain yogurt**

Sauté onion and garlic in butter; add spinach and sauté until heated through. Transfer to a serving bowl and cool to lukewarm. Add yogurt and mix well. Chill for at least 2 hours before serving. **Makes about 2 cups.**

HUMMUS

1   **16-ounce can chickpeas, drained**
2   **tablespoons tahini (ground sesame-seed paste)**
Juice of ½ lemon (about 2 tablespoons)
2   **cloves garlic, mashed**
Olive oil

Combine chickpeas, tahini, lemon juice, and garlic in work bowl of food processor or blender and process until smooth. Transfer mixture to a serving bowl, drizzle olive oil over the top, cover, and chill. Use as a sandwich filling or dip. **Makes about 2 cups.**

SOUPS

Hot or cold, soups are a welcome and nutritious addition to any meal. Almost everything is good about soup; it's economical to make, easy to prepare, and makes for satisfying eating.

COLD AVOCADO SOUP

4   **medium ripe avocados, sliced, peeled, and pitted**
2   **quarts chicken broth, homemade or canned**
¹/₂   **medium onion, coarsely chopped**
1   **tablespoon chopped fresh coriander** (*cilantro* in Latin American stores)
Juice of 1 lemon

Put avocados, 1 cup broth, onion, coriander, and lemon juice in work bowl of blender or food processor and process until smooth. Add remaining broth and process until thoroughly blended. Chill well before serving. **Serves 6 to 8.**

BEAN SPROUT SOUP

12 ounces bean sprouts
4 tablespoons butter
3 cups chicken broth, homemade or canned
6 slices toasted French or Italian bread
1 cup grated cheddar cheese

Preheat oven to 275° F. Gently cook bean sprouts in butter until well browned; transfer to a medium casserole. Add chicken broth, top with toasted bread, and sprinkle cheese over all. Bake until cheese is melted, about 10 minutes. **Makes 6 ½-cup servings.**

CREAM OF BROCCOLI SOUP

Since the broccoli is poached directly in the stock without prior steaming, nothing is lost in the way of precious vitamins or flavor.

1 bunch broccoli, washed, trimmed, and broken into florets
2 cups chicken stock, homemade or canned
2½ tablespoons all-purpose flour
¾ cup light cream
   A generous pinch of thyme

Poach broccoli in chicken stock until very tender. In a small bowl, combine flour and cream, adding a little hot broth to form a paste. Add flour mixture to broccoli, stirring constantly until well blended and slightly thickened. Do not allow to boil. Just before serving, stir in thyme. **Serves 6.**

CREAM OF CAULIFLOWER SOUP

Follow method above, substituting 1 head cauliflower for the broccoli.

COLD CUCUMBER SOUP

2 **large cucumbers, peeled, seeded, and quartered**
1 **large clove garlic**
2 **scallions, including tops**
1 **bunch fresh dill**
1 **cup plain yogurt**

Puree cucumbers, garlic, and scallions in work bowl of blender or food processor. Add dill and process a few seconds more. Blend in yogurt and chill thoroughly before serving. **Serves 4.**

QUICK EGG DROP SOUP

4   cups chicken broth, homemade or canned

1½ cups shredded Chinese cabbage (*bok choy*) or other greens, optional

2   scallions, coarsely diced

2   tablespoons soy sauce

2   eggs, lightly beaten

In a medium saucepan over moderate heat, combine broth, cabbage, and scallions and cook until vegetables are tender. Stir in soy sauce. Add eggs, a little at a time, stirring constantly. Heat thoroughly and serve. **Serves 6 to 8.**

LEMON-RICE SOUP

This soup is very similar to Stracciatella (see page 27). A little bit of lemon and leftover rice make the difference.

1   egg yolk
2   tablespoons lemon juice
6   tablespoons grated Parmesan cheese
6   cups hot chicken broth, homemade or
     canned
1   cup cooked rice

Mix egg yolk, lemon juice and Parmesan cheese together in a small bowl. Add mixture to hot broth, stirring constantly. Add rice and simmer 3 to 4 minutes. Do not boil. **Serves 6.**

RAW ONION SOUP

All the flavor of cooked onion soups—but half the work.

1   quart milk
3   large onions, sliced thin
Dash nutmeg
Salt and freshly ground pepper to taste

In a medium saucepan, heat milk to boiling; pour over sliced onions, and allow to steep 20 minutes, pressing onions occasionally with the back of a spoon to squeeze juice from them. Strain milk back into saucepan; add nutmeg and salt and pepper to taste. Heat and serve. **Serves 6.**

OYSTER STEW

The traditional fare for Christmas Eve.

2 **tablespoons butter**
$1/2$ **pint fresh shucked oysters, with liquid**
1 **cup clam broth, homemade or canned**
Salt and freshly ground pepper to taste
1 **cup light cream**

Melt butter in a medium, heavy saucepan. Add oysters, broth, salt, and pepper. Simmer over low heat 10 minutes; add cream and heat very hot, making sure stew does not boil. Place a dot of butter in each soup bowl before serving, and garnish with additional fresh pepper, if desired. **Serves 4.**

SALMON BISQUE

2 **tablespoons butter**
$1/2$ **cup chopped onions**
2 **tablespoons all-purpose flour**
4 **cups milk**
2 **7-ounce cans salmon, drained and finely chopped**

In a medium saucepan, heat butter; add onion and cook until limp but not browned. Add flour and $2/3$ cup milk and bring to a boil, stirring constantly. Gradually add remaining milk and salmon. Cook until smooth and slightly thickened. Season with salt and pepper if desired. **Serves 6.**

STRACCIATELLA

3 **eggs**
1/4 **cup grated Parmesan cheese**
2 **tablespoons all-purpose flour**
2 **quarts hot chicken broth, homemade or canned**

Beat eggs, cheese, and flour in a small bowl. Add mixture to hot broth, whisking constantly. Simmer 3 to 4 minutes. Do not boil. **Serves 6.**

COLD STRAWBERRY SOUP

Perfect for a summer lunch. The addition of kirsch really brings out the flavor of the fruit.

1 **quart strawberries, washed and hulled**
1 **quart buttermilk**
3/4 **cup sugar**
2/3 **cup sour cream**
3 **tablespoons kirsch**

Place berries in work bowl of food processor or blender with 1 cup buttermilk and sugar. Process until smooth. Pour into a soup tureen. Combine sour cream, remaining buttermilk, and kirsch in work bowl and process 3 to 4 seconds; add to strawberries. Serve well chilled. **Serves 6 to 8.**

VICHYSSOISE

2   **pounds leeks, washed, trimmed, and thinly sliced**
2   **pounds potatoes, pceled and diced**
2   **quarts chicken stock, homemade or canned**
3³/₄   **cups light cream or half and half**
   Snipped fresh chivcs

Place leeks and potatoes in a large, heavy saucepan and add enough chicken stock to cover. Cover and simmer until vegetables are very tender. Remove from pan and puree, a little at a time, in work bowl of blender or food processor. Return puree to saucepan over low heat; add cream, stirring constantly, until blended. Chill until ready to serve and garnish with snipped chives. Season with salt and pepper if desired. **Serves 6 to 8.**

WATERCRESS SOUP

2 cups watercress, cleaned and trimmed
1 pound potatoes, peeled and sliced
1 tablespoon salt
1 cup milk
4 slices French bread, cut ½ inch thick

In a large saucepan combine watercress, potatoes, salt, and 6 cups water. Bring to a boil, cover, and simmer 30 minutes, or until potatoes are tender. Strain vegetables and reserve liquid. Place vegetables in work bowl of food processor or blender and puree. Return puree to pan, add reserved vegetable liquid, and bring to a boil. Lower heat, whisk in remaining milk, and cook until heated through. Do not boil. Place one slice of bread on bottom of each soup plate. Pour hot soup over. **Serves 4.**

WHITE WINE SOUP

6 cups white wine
4 tablespoons sugar
3 egg yolks
Croutons

Place egg yolks in the bottom of a soup tureen and beat lightly with a fork. In a medium saucepan, bring wine and sugar to a boil and boil 5 minutes. Gradually pour hot mixture over yolks, whisking constantly. Top with croutons and serve immediately. **Serves 3 to 4.**

CURRIED ZUCCHINI SOUP

Vary the amount of curry according to taste—not too much, though, or it will overpower the fresh taste of the zucchini.

8 **medium zucchini, washed, ends trimmed, and cut into thick slices**
4 **cups chicken broth, homemade or canned**
2 **medium onions, chopped**
1 **tablespoon curry powder, or to taste**
1¹/₂ **cups milk or cream**

Place zucchini in a medium saucepan with chicken broth, onion, and curry. Cover and simmer until vegetables are tender, stirring occasionally. Pour mixture into work bowl of food processor or blender. (You may need to do this in several batches.) Puree until smooth. Return puree to saucepan, add milk and heat. Do not boil. **Serves 8.**

EASY
EXOTICS

HUNGARIAN BREAD SOUP

A peasant soup that is not only economical but hearty and satisfying. Served with a salad or vegetable, it makes a great winter supper.

6	**thick slices bacon, diced**
6	**thick slices stale bread, cut into cubes**
2½	**cups beef stock, homemade or canned**
1	**tablespoon paprika, or to taste**
3	**eggs, beaten**

Fry bacon until transparent. Add bread cubes and continue frying until bacon is very crisp and bread cubes are golden. In a medium saucepan, combine beef stock and 2 cups boiling water. Return to a boil. Add bread cubes and bacon. Season with paprika. When soup is boiling vigorously, add eggs in a thin stream, stirring constantly. Serve immediately. **Serves 5 to 6.**

CHRYSANTHEMUM SOUP

Though our original recipe called for fresh chrysanthemum petals, it's best to use the dried variety available in Japanese markets. Some kinds of American chrysanthemum are poisonous, so unless you're a botanist as as a cook use dried!

2 large Japanese mushrooms, sliced
3 cups chicken broth, homemade or canned, heated
¼ cup dry sherry
2 teaspoons light soy sauce
1 package dried Japanese chrysanthemum petals

Soak mushrooms in heated broth for several hours; strain broth and reserve. Slice mushrooms into very small strips, discarding any hard stems. Combine reserved broth with sherry and soy sauce, add mushrooms and simmer about 10 minutes over low heat. Immediately before serving, add petals, stir, and ladle into bowls. **Serves 4.**

CREAM OF COCONUT SOUP
(Sopa de crema de coco)

1 medium onion, grated
2 tablespoons butter
2 tablespoons all-purpose flour
1 quart chicken stock, homemade or canned
1 15-ounce can unsweetened coconut milk, or use the recipe on page 33 to make 1¼ cups

Sauté onion in butter until soft. Add flour to make a roux and cook 2 to 3 minutes. Meanwhile, in a 2-quart saucepan, heat stock to boiling. Add a little hot stock to the roux; blend and add to stock. Add 2 tablespoons coconut milk to heated stock; cover and simmer 15 minutes, or until slightly thickened. Add remainder of coconut milk, stir to blend, and continue to cook until soup is heated through. Do not allow to boil. **Serves 6 to 8.**

FRESH COCONUT MILK
1   coconut

Preheat oven to 400° F. Check to make sure coconut has enough liquid by shaking it. With a nail, or other sharp instrument, pierce two of the three eyes on top of the coconut; drain liquid and reserve. Bake coconut for 15 minutes. On a hard surface, crack the shell with a hammer; the shell should fall away easily. When making coconut milk, it is not necessary to remove the brown inner skin. Break coconut into small chunks, and place in work bowl of food processor or blender. Process until finely grated. Place coconut in a cheesecloth and squeeze out all liquid. Grate again and repeat. Discard coconut, and combine the thick milk with reserved liquid. **Makes about 1¼ cups.**

HEARTS OF PALM SOUP

2   tablespoons rice flour or cornstarch
1   cup milk
1   14-ounce can hearts of palm, drained
     and chopped
5   cups chicken stock, homemade or
     canned
2   egg yolks, beaten

In a 2-quart saucepan, combine rice flour with milk.
Puree hearts of palm together with 1 cup of stock in
work bowl of blender or food processor. Add to saucepan with remaining stock and cook, stirring constantly,
over low heat until soup is smooth and slightly thickened. Add a little hot soup to egg yolks, then pour egg
yolk mixture into soup. Cook, stirring constantly, about
2 minutes. Do not allow to boil. **Serves 6.**

CREAM OF PEANUT SOUP

1   tablespoon butter
$\frac{1}{2}$ small onion, chopped
1   tablespoon all-purpose flour
1   quart milk
$\frac{1}{2}$ cup peanut butter

In a small skillet, melt butter; add onion and sauté until golden. Add flour to make a roux and cook 2 to 3 minutes. In a medium saucepan, bring milk to a boil. Reduce heat. Pour a small amount of hot milk into roux, and stir until blended. Add roux to remaining milk, whisking constantly. Return to heat, add peanut butter, and continue to whisk until ingredients are heated through. **Serves 4.**

PLANTAIN SOUP

1   **green plantain, about 1 pound**
5   **cups chicken stock, homemade or canned**
Salt and freshly ground pepper to taste

Peel plantain and puree in work bowl of food processor or blender. Add plantain to cold stock, cover and place over medium heat, stirring occasionally, until soup is thickened, about 45 minutes. Season to taste with salt and pepper and simmer an additional 15 minutes. **Serves 4 to 6.**

The
Main
Event

Here's your chance to really show off. The entrée or main dish in any meal should be a special effort, one that is complemented by your choice of side dishes and vegetables. Some of the recipes included here are familiar, for those days when you have that special craving for something simple, wholesome, and good, while others are more elaborate—giving you a chance to really display your talents as a creative cook. But whatever your choices for your main event, we guarantee no one would ever guess how simple these recipes really are.

Beef and Veal

BEEF WITH LEMON

2 pounds of beef sirloin, well trimmed and cut into 2-inch cubes
3 tablespoons olive oil
2 cloves garlic, minced
$\frac{1}{4}$ to $\frac{1}{3}$ cup lemon juice, or to taste
1 teaspoon Italian seasoning

Combine all ingredients in a large bowl and marinate in the refrigerator 2 to 3 hours. Thread beef on skewers and barbecue over charcoal or broil. **Serves 4.**

BEEF FILLET WITH OYSTERS AND CREAM

1³/₄ pounds beef fillet
2   dozen oysters, shucked, liquid
     reserved
1   cup heavy cream
2   egg yolks
3   tablespoons butter

Broil beef fillets according to preference. Meanwhile, poach shucked oysters in their liquid just until tender. Remove oysters and reduce liquid to a glaze over medium high heat. Add butter to the pan and melt. In a small bowl beat together cream and egg yolk. Add a little hot glaze to egg-yolk mixture. Add egg-yolk mixture and oysters to pan; blend well until slightly thickened over low heat. Serve oyster sauce over beef. **Serves 4.**

BOILED DINNER

1   3- to 4-pound corned beef brisket
1   medium cabbage, cut into chunks
6   turnips, quartered
6   small potatoes
6   small carrots

In a 4-quart saucepan, cover beef with cold water and slowly bring to a boil, skimming off the fat as it accumulates. Reduce heat; cover and simmer 3 hours, or until beef is tender. Add vegetables; simmer an additional 45 minutes, or until done. Arrange beef in the center of a serving platter surrounded by vegetables. **Serves 6.**

ITALIAN CHUCK STEAK

1   2½-pound center-cut chuck steak, 2½ inches thick
3   cloves garlic, crushed
1   16-ounce can tomatoes
2   teaspoons Italian seasoning
½   green pepper, seeded and cut into 1-inch chunks

Preheat oven to 325° F. Place all ingredients in a roasting pan and cover with pan lid or aluminum foil. Roast 1¼ hours. Increase heat to 350° F. Uncover and roast an additional 15 minutes to brown. **Serves 4.**

SHERRIED LONDON BROIL

Always slice London broil across the grain, as it serves to tenderize the meat.

1   2 to 3 pound London broil or top round
    steak

MARINADE

1   cup dry sherry
1   cup chopped onion
2   garlic cloves, crushed
4   tablespoons sesame oil

Combine marinade ingredients in a large flat pan. Add
meat and marinate in refrigerator 3 to 4 hours, turning
occasionally. Remove pan from refrigerator and bring
meat to room temperature. Broil 7 minutes on each side
for rare, adding three minutes per pound for medium.
To serve, carve horizontally across the grain into paper-
thin slices. **Serves 6 to 8.**

MIXED GRILL

$\frac{1}{2}$ pound sirloin steak, cut into 2-inch
    cubes
$\frac{1}{4}$ pound calf's liver, sliced
4   chorizo or kielbasa sausages cut into
    1-inch pieces
4   small onions, halved
$\frac{1}{2}$ pound large fresh mushrooms

Thread meat and vegetables alternately onto 4 metal skewers, 6 inches long. Barbecue over charcoal or broil. **Serves 4.**

POT ROAST WITH BOURBON

If you like, add your choice of vegetables and potatoes.

    1   **3- to 4-pound boneless chuck roast**
    1   **tablespoon oregano**
    1   **tablespoon basil**
    6   **slices bacon**
    1   **cup bourbon**

Preheat oven to 350° F. Cut 6 slits, about 1 inch deep, into top of roast. Combine herbs in a small bowl; add bacon slices to herb mixture and combine until well coated. Roll up the bacon and stuff one slice into each slit. Pour bourbon over all. Place roast in pan, cover, and roast approximately 2 hours, or until meat is very tender. **Serves 4 to 6.**

ROAST BEEF WITH YORKSHIRE PUDDING

1   4- to 5-pound beef roast, sirloin tip or
    top round
1   cup all-purpose flour
1   teaspoon salt
2   eggs, beaten
3/4 cup milk
1/2 cup water

Preheat oven to 425° F. Roast the beef, uncovered, for
20 minutes. Lower oven temperature to 375° F and continue to roast for 1 hour and 15 minutes for medium,
basting frequently. Meanwhile, sift flour and salt together in a medium bowl. Make a well in the center,
add eggs, and stir. Add milk and water and beat to make
a smooth batter. When roast is done, remove to a serving
platter and keep warm. Pour pudding batter into roasting pan; return to oven and bake 30 minutes, or until
pudding is risen and golden. **Serves 6.**

STEAK MARINADE

1¹/₂ pounds good quality chuck steak, cut
      1¹/₂ inches thick
¹/₂   cup soy sauce
¹/₂   cup cream sherry
2   tablespoons tahini (sesame paste)
2   cloves garlic, crushed

Cut steak into serving pieces. Combine soy sauce, sherry, tahini, and garlic and pour over steak. Marinate in refrigerator 2 to 3 hours. Transfer to broiler pan and broil according to preference. **Serves 4 to 6.**

FIVE-INGREDIENT CHILI

A great basic chili recipe. Serve with an assortment of garnishes if you like—chopped scallions, shredded cheese, or sour cream are always great. Serve additional Tabasco sauce for those who like it very hot.

1½   **pounds ground chuck**

2   **large onions, chopped**

1   **28-ounce can tomatoes in tomato puree**

1   **15-ounce can chili beans (kidney beans will do), undrained**

4 to 5   **tablespoons chili seasoning, or to taste**

Brown meat and onions together in a large skillet. Add undrained tomatoes and beans and half of seasoning. Simmer over low heat 2 hours or until sauce is reduced and slightly thickened. A half hour before serving add the remaining seasoning and continue to simmer, stirring occasionally. **Serves 4 to 6.**

HAMBURGERS MEXICALI

1½ pounds ground beef
1 tablespoon freeze-dried chives
1 envelope chili-seasoning mix
1 ripe avocado, cut into 6 slices

In a medium bowl, combine the beef, chives, and seasoning by tossing together lightly. Shape into 6 large patties. Pan fry, broil, or grill over charcoal. Top with a slice of avocado. **Serves 6.**

EASY MEATBALLS

1 pound lean ground beef
1 egg
2 cloves garlic
1 tablespoon Italian seasoning
½ cup cracker crumbs

Combine all ingredients in a medium bowl and shape into small balls, about 1½ inch in diameter. Brown evenly over medium high heat, turning frequently. Serve alone or with any tomato sauce. **Serves 4.**

SHERRIED LIVER

1   **pound calf's liver, cut into 8 equal slices**
    Seasoned flour
$^1/_4$ **cup butter**
1   **medium onion, chopped**
$^1/_2$ **cup dry sherry**

Wipe liver slices with a damp cloth or paper toweling. Dredge in seasoned flour. Melt butter in a medium skillet and add chopped onion. Sauté until golden. Add liver slices and sauté 2 to 3 minutes over medium high heat. Turn slices and sauté 1 more minute or until juices run pink and the second side is browned. Remove to a serving platter. Add sherry to pan drippings and swirl to deglaze the pan. Simmer until sherry is reduced by one-third and sauce is slightly thickened. Pour sauce over liver to serve. **Serves 4.**

LIVER MARSALA

Follow procedure for sherried liver, substituting 1 teaspoon dried rosemary for onion and $^1/_2$ cup Marsala for the sherry.

LIVER IN
SOUR CREAM GRAVY

Even people who hate liver like this.

4	**strips bacon**
1	**pound calf's liver, cut into 8 equal slices**
½	**cup seasoned flour**
1	**medium onion, thinly sliced**
½	**cup sour cream**

Fry bacon until very crisp. Remove from pan, drain, and crumble. Dredge liver slices in seasoned flour; add to pan and sauté 2 to 3 minutes over medium high heat. Turn slices and sauté 1 more minute or until juices run pink and the second side is browned. Remove liver to serving platter and keep warm. Add onion to pan and sauté until golden; add sour cream and heat through. Pour onion–sour-cream sauce over liver and garnish with crumbled bacon. **Serves 4.**

VEAL WITH APPLES

The most important thing to remember about cooking veal is not to overcook it. Veal scallops, pounded thin, should be sautéed only a few minutes on each side.

1½   pounds veal scallops, cut ³/₈ -inch thick
     and pounded to ¼ inch.
Seasoned flour
6   tablespoons butter
2   Cortland or McIntosh apples (a
     crisp, firm variety is best), peeled,
     cored, and sliced
1   cup heavy cream

Dredge veal scallops in flour. In a medium skillet, melt butter; add veal scallops, a few at a time. Do not let them overlap in the pan. Sauté 2 to 3 minutes on each side over medium heat. Remove to serving platter. Add sliced apples to pan, and sauté until lightly browned. Add cream and continue cooking over medium heat until sauce is reduced by half. Pour apple-cream sauce over veal scallops and garnish with additional apple slices, if desired. **Serves 4.**

VEAL PAPRIKASH

1½   pounds stewing veal, cut into 1-inch
     cubes
½   cup seasoned flour
½   cup butter
1½   tablespoons Hungarian rose paprika,
     or to taste
1   cup sour cream

Dredge veal in seasoned flour. In a large skillet, melt butter until foaming. Add veal and sauté until lightly browned on all sides. Reduce heat and add paprika, stirring until veal is well coated. Add 1 cup water and cook, covered, over low heat for 30 minutes, or until veal is very tender. Add sour cream and continue cooking until sauce is heated through. **Serves 4 to 6.**

VEAL PICCANTE

$1^1\!/_2$ **pounds veal scallops, cut $^3\!/_8$ -inch thick
      and pounded to $^1\!/_4$ inch**
      Seasoned flour
$^1\!/_4$ **cup butter**
2   **teaspoons capers**
$^1\!/_4$ **cup brandy**

Dredge veal scallops in seasoned flour. Melt butter in a medium skillet; add scallops, a few at a time. Do not let them overlap in the pan. Sauté 2 to 3 minutes on each side over medium heat. Remove scallops to a serving platter. Add capers to pan juices. Add brandy and ignite to burn off alcohol. Heat thoroughly; pour sauce over veal scallops. **Serves 4.**

VEAL PICCATA

1½   pounds veal scallops, sliced ⅜-inch
     thick and pounded to ¼ inch
½   cup butter
⅔   cup seasoned flour
     Juice of 1 lemon
¼   cup chopped fresh parsley

Dredge veal scallops in seasoned flour. In a large skillet over medium heat, melt butter until foaming. Add veal scallops, making sure they do not overlap, and sauté 3 minutes on each side. Reduce heat and add lemon juice and parsley. Cook until parsley is limp. **Serves 4.**

VEAL CHOPS STROGANOFF

4   veal chops, ½ to ¾ inches thick
     Seasoned flour
¼   cup butter or margarine
1   cup sour cream
¼   cup white wine

Dredge chops in seasoned flour and sauté in butter over medium heat, about 4 minutes on each side. Add cream and wine and simmer, uncovered, over low heat until sauce is reduced and slightly thickened. **Serves 4.**

EASY

EXOTICS

WOODEN PLATE

A Hungarian version of a mixed grill.

1   **pound sirloin, cut into 2-inch pieces**
1   **pound veal cutlets, cut into 2-inch pieces**
1   **pound calf's liver, cut into 2-inch pieces**
6   **strips thick-sliced bacon, diced**
6   **new potatoes, sliced thin**

Place sirloin, veal, and liver on a broiler pan and place about 6 inches under broiler. Cook 10 minutes, turning pieces to brown. Meanwhile, in a heavy skillet, fry the bacon until lightly crisp; add potato slices and continue frying until potatoes are cooked through and nicely browned. Serve meats on a bed of fried potatoes. Top with diced bacon. **Serves 6.**

LAMB AND PORK

COLA LEG OF LAMB

For those with a sweet tooth.

1   **5-pound leg of lamb**
Coarse sea salt
Freshly ground pepper
2   **cloves garlic, quartered**
1   **cup cola**

Preheat oven to 400° F. Rub lamb with salt and pepper. Cut slits about 2 inches apart in fat and insert garlic. Place in a roasting pan and pour cola over. Cover with pan lid or aluminum foil. Bake for 25 minutes. Reduce oven temperature to 325° F and continue roasting uncovered, basting frequently, for 1 hour or longer, depending on preference. **Serves 6.**

DIJON LAMB

4   loin lamb chops, about 2 inches thick
1½   tablespoons Dijon mustard
2   cloves garlic, crushed
3   tablespoons butter
1   tablespoon chopped fresh tarragon, or
1   teaspoon dried tarragon

Preheat oven to broil. Make a slit in each chop lengthwise to form a pocket. Combine remaining ingredients to make a paste. Tuck an equal portion of the butter-tarragon mixture into each chop and broil 10 minutes on each side for medium. **Serves 4.**

RUSSIAN LAMB KEBABS

2   pounds boneless lamb, cut into 2-inch cubes
1   large eggplant, peeled and cut into 2-inch chunks
2   tablespoons butter
2   large tomatoes, sliced
Freshly ground pepper

Preheat oven to 350° F. Thread lamb and eggplant alternately onto 6-inch metal skewers. Sauté into melted butter until golden brown. Place skewers in a shallow baking dish and cover with overlapping slices of tomato. Sprinkle with freshly ground pepper and bake 30 minutes. **Serves 4.**

SWISS LAMB

Don't substitute canned mushrooms for fresh. The taste just isn't the same.

> 4   **loin lamb chops, cut 2 inches thick**
> 2   **cups chopped fresh mushrooms**
> 4   **tablespoons butter**
> 1/4 **cup dry sherry**
> 1   **cup grated Swiss cheese**

Preheat oven to broil. Broil lamb chops about 10 minutes on each side for medium. Meanwhile, sauté mushrooms in butter, add sherry, and cook until sauce is slightly reduced. Top each chop with a generous portion of the mushroom-sherry mixture, and heap grated cheese over all. Place in a shallow broiler pan and broil 1 to 2 minutes more, or until cheese is melted. **Serves 4.**

HAM AND CHEESE KEBOBS

This makes a quick delicious lunch or light supper. Serve with Baked Potato Chips (see page 108) and a green salad.

1   **pound Jarlsberg cheese, cut into 16 1-inch chunks**
8   **slices boiled ham, cut in half**
2   **eggs, lightly beaten**
1   **cup seasoned bread crumbs**
    Oil for deep frying

Wrap each cheese chunk in ½ slice ham. Thread 4 wrapped cheese chunks onto 4 6-inch skewers. Dip skewers in egg, then roll in bread crumbs. Repeat, making sure cheese chunks are well coated. Heat oil for deep frying to 375° F and fry just until golden. **Serves 4.**

HONEY-GLAZED HAM

½   **cup honey**
¼   **cup ground walnuts**
½   **cup chicken broth**
1   **tablespoon Dijon mustard**
1   **5- to 6-pound fully cooked ham, butt portion**

Preheat oven to 350° F. Combine honey, walnuts, broth, and mustard until well blended. Brush mixture over ham and bake 1½ hours, basting occasionally, until glaze is well browned and fat is crispy. Serve glaze as a dipping sauce. **Serves 8 to 10.**

SCALLOPED POTATOES WITH HAM

6   slices baked ham, ¼ to ½ inch thick
4   medium baking potatoes, scrubbed and thinly sliced
1   medium onion, thinly sliced
2   tablespoons all-purpose flour
1   cup half and half

Preheat oven to 400° F. Layer ham, potatoes, and onion in baking dish. Combine flour with a small amount of half and half to make a paste, then add the rest of the half and half. Pour over casserole and bake approximately 40 minutes, or until potatoes are tender and casserole is lightly browned. **Serves 4.**

ROAST PORK AND GRAVY

1   4- to 5-pound pork loin roast
4   garlic cloves, peeled and cut in thirds
    Coarse sea salt
1 to 2   tablespoons Worcestershire sauce
1   tablespoon all-purpose flour

Preheat oven to 425° F. Place roast, fat side up, in a roasting pan and rub fat thoroughly with salt. Cut slits about 2 inches apart in the roast's fat and insert garlic. Cook approximately 40 minutes to the pound, adding a little water from time to time to keep drippings from scorching. When roast is done, remove from pan and keep warm. Skim fat, then add ½ cup water to pan drippings. Place roasting pan directly over a low flame and boil, scraping bottom of pan to loosen drippings. Add 1 tablespoon Worcestershire sauce to pan drippings and stir. Slowly add ¼ cup cold water to 1 tablespoon flour and blend to make a thin paste. Add to pan and cook, stirring constantly, until thickened. Add more Worcestershire sauce to taste. **Serves 6 to 8.**

ITALIAN PORK ROAST

1   4-pound pork loin roast
8 to 10   cloves garlic, halved
1 to 2   tablespoons fennel seed
    Coarse sea salt
    Freshly ground black pepper

Cut about 20 slits into the fatty portion of the roast, and into each slit tuck ½ clove of garlic and a few fennel seeds. Rub entire roast well with salt and pepper. Cover with aluminum foil and refrigerate overnight. Bring roast to room temperature before placing in a preheated 350° F oven. Roast approximately 30 minutes to the pound. **Serves 6 to 8.**

NOTE: For a variation of the above recipe, substitute 1 tablespoon caraway seeds for fennel.

PINEAPPLE PORK CHOPS

6 **center-cut pork chops, well trimmed**
1 **8-ounce can crushed pineapple, undrained**
2 **tablespoons brown sugar**
¼ **cup wine vinegar**
¼ **cup honey**

Trim off excess fat from pork chops and place in a large skillet over medium heat. When fat begins to sizzle, add chops and cook 2 to 3 minutes on each side, or until lightly browned. Remove fat pieces and pour off any excess fat. Combine remaining ingredients in a small bowl and mix until well blended. Pour over chops; cover, and cook 20 to 30 minutes over medium heat, turning chops occasionally. **Serves 6.**

PORK CHOPS WITH WINE SAUCE

4 **loin pork chops, cut ½ to ¾ inch thick**
½ **teaspoon freshly ground pepper**
⅓ **cup olive oil**
2 **large garlic cloves, minced**
¾ **dry red wine**

Rub chops well with freshly ground pepper. In a medium skillet, heat oil very hot; add chops and sear over high heat until brown, about 4 minutes on each side. Pour off all but 3 tablespoons oil and add garlic. Cover skillet, reduce heat, and cook chops until very tender, about 30 minutes, turning occasionally. Remove chops to a serving platter and keep warm. Add wine to pan, stirring to loosen drippings. Bring to a boil and cook until sauce is reduced by half. Pour sauce over chops and serve. **Serves 4.**

EASY

EXOTICS

CASSEROLE SHASHLIK

Shish kebab without skewers . . .

$3^{1}/_{2}$ **pounds boneless lamb, cut into $1^{1}/_{2}$-inch cubes**

2   **large onions, sliced**

$^{3}/_{4}$ **cup raisins**

1   **teaspoon whole coriander seeds, or 4 teaspoons powdered coriander**

$^{1}/_{2}$ **teaspoon turmeric**

Preheat oven to 325° F. Place cubed lamb in the bottom of a $1^{1}/_{2}$-quart casserole. Top with sliced onions and raisins; sprinkle with spices. Cover and bake until lamb is very tender, 1 to $1^{1}/_{2}$ hours. **Serves 6.**

POLISH STEW

2   **pounds kielbasa sausage, cut into 2-inch pieces**

3   **large white onions, cut into chunks**

4   **medium zucchini, sliced**

5   **large tomatoes, cut into eighths**

In a large saucepan over moderate heat, sauté a few pieces of sausage until they give off enough fat to grease the pan. Add remaining sausage and vegetables and cook for 30 minutes, stirring occasionally. **Serves 6 to 8.**

PORK LOIN IN MILK

Cooking meats in milk is practiced all over the world as a means of tenderizing, as well as imparting a delicious flavor of its own.

Salt and freshly ground pepper to taste
3   pounds boneless pork loin
2   tablespoons butter
3   cups milk

Preheat oven to 375° F. Rub pork loin with salt and freshly ground pepper. In a roasting pan or casserole, melt butter, add pork loin and brown over high heat on all sides. Remove from heat. Pour milk over and bake, covered, for 2 hours, or until roast is very tender and sauce is reduced and slightly thickened. **Serves 6.**

NOTE: The above recipe is Italian in origin, but exists in a number of different versions. For the Latin American variation, add the juice of one lemon to the milk before adding to roast. This clabbers the milk slightly, and makes for a more piquant and thicker sauce.

POULTRY

CHICKEN IN CHAMPAGNE

No need to use expensive champagne, save that to drink!

1   **3-pound frying chicken, quartered**
4   **tablespoons butter**
³/₄   **cup champagne**
1   **cup heavy cream**
1   **egg yolk, lightly beaten**

Sauté chicken in butter until tender, about 30 minutes. Remove to serving platter. Add champagne to pan, scraping up bits of drippings. Add ²/₃ cup of cream and simmer over low heat until sauce is reduced by a third. Beat remaining cream and egg yolk together. Add a little hot champagne sauce to egg yolk; then add to saucepan, stirring constantly over low heat until slightly thickened. Pour over chicken to serve. **Serves 4.**

CHICKEN BREASTS FLORENTINE

2   whole chicken breasts, boned, skinned and pounded to $1/4$-inch thickness
$1/2$ cup seasoned flour
$1/2$ cup butter
A generous splash of sherry
$1/2$ pound fresh spinach, shredded

Dredge chicken breasts in seasoned flour. Over moderate heat sauté in butter until very tender. Transfer chicken to a warm platter and set aside. Add sherry to pan juices. Add shredded spinach and sauté until limp. Top each breast portion with equal amounts of spinach and serve. **Serves 4.**

CHICKEN WITH GARLIC

Don't be put off by the amount of garlic called for in this recipe. The garlic actually acquires a gentle, almost sweet taste during baking which is delicious.

1   4-pound roasting chicken
40   garlic cloves, unpeeled
$1/2$ cup dry white wine
1   cup half and half

Preheat oven to 350° F. Place chicken, wine, and garlic in a tightly covered roasting pan and bake 2 hours, or until chicken is very tender. When done, remove chicken from pan and keep warm; transfer garlic to a separate dish. Add half and half to pan drippings. Place roasting pan directly over low heat and simmer gently, stirring to loosen drippings. Peel garlic by gently squeezing pulp out of skin. Puree or mash garlic and add to roasting pan. Serve garlic sauce as an accompaniment to chicken. **Serves 4 to 6.**

EASY CHICKEN KIEV

2   **whole chicken breasts, skinned, boned, and split**
½   **cup butter, well chilled**
2   **eggs, beaten**
1   **cup seasoned bread crumbs**
Oil for deep frying

Pound chicken breasts to ¼-inch thickness. Cut butter into 4 equal portions. Place one portion in the center of each chicken breast; roll up breast and secure with toothpicks. Dip each roll into beaten egg, then roll in bread crumbs. Repeat. Allow chicken rolls to dry in refrigerator at least 2 hours before frying. Heat oil over moderately high heat; add chicken rolls and fry until golden, approximately 12 minutes. **Serves 4.**

LEMON CHICKEN

1   3¹/₂-pound frying chicken, cut into
serving pieces
2   lemons, sliced
2   tablespoons dried oregano
Salt and freshly ground pepper to taste

Preheat oven to 425° F. Wash chicken and pat dry. Arrange lemon slices in the bottom of a baking dish. Combine oregano and salt and pepper and rub thoroughly over chicken pieces. Place chicken pieces, skin side down, over lemon. Bake 20 minutes. Turn chicken skin side up; reduce heat to 350° F and continue cooking 35 minutes longer or until chicken is very tender. **Serves 4 to 6.**

ORIENTAL BARBECUED CHICKEN

Serve with sautéed snow pea pods and mushrooms.

1   2- to 3-pound frying chicken, cut into
serving pieces.
¹/₂   cup soy sauce
¹/₄   cup honey
1   tablespoon grated fresh gingerroot
2   cloves garlic, crushed

Marinate chicken pieces in soy sauce, honey, ginger, and garlic for at least 2 hours. Place under broiler or barbecue over charcoal until tender, basting occasionally with remaining marinade. **Serves 4.**

CHICKEN WITH PEARS

Serve this dish hot for dinner, or refrigerate at least 2 hours for a wonderful cold lunch.

2   **cups chicken broth**
2   **ripe pears**
2   **whole chicken breasts, skinned, boned, and halved**
1   **cup heavy cream**
Freshly ground pepper

In a medium saucepan, bring broth to a simmer. Peel and core pears, reserving peel. Poach pears in broth until tender, then transfer pears to work bowl of food processor or blender and puree. Add chicken to simmering broth with pear peelings and poach until chicken is tender. Remove from heat. In a small saucepan, boil cream until reduced to approximately ½ cup. Add pear puree and heat through. Transfer chicken pieces to a serving platter. Pour pear sauce over and garnish with freshly ground pepper. **Serves 4.**

CHICKEN AND SAUSAGE BAKE

1   2- to 3-pound frying chicken, cut into serving pieces
1   pound sweet Italian sausage, cut into 2-inch pieces
1   16-ounce can tomatoes
2   cloves garlic, minced
1   sweet green pepper, cut into chunks

Preheat oven to 375° F. Lightly sauté chicken and sausage in a large oven-proof casserole until browned. Add tomatoes, garlic, and green pepper. Bake, covered, 1½ hours, or until broth is somewhat reduced and chicken is tender. **Serves 4.**

SCOTCH CHICKEN

4   tablespoons butter, softened
3   tablespoons Dijon mustard
1   2- to 3-pound frying chicken, quartered
¼   cup Scotch whisky
⅓   cup heavy cream

Mix butter and mustard together to form a paste; spread over chicken. Over moderate heat sauté chicken on both sides until lightly browned. Cover and simmer about 30 minutes. Add Scotch and allow to warm slightly. Ignite and burn off alcohol. Add cream and continue to simmer, uncovered, 10 to 12 minutes or until sauce has reduced slightly. Do not allow to boil. **Serves 4.**

BOURBON CHICKEN

Follow the above recipe, substituting ¼ cup sour mash bourbon for the Scotch.

SHERRIED CHICKEN

1	**3-pound broiling chicken, split lengthwise**
1	**cup thinly sliced onion**
½	**cup butter, melted**
1½	**cups dry sherry**
1	**cup fresh mushroom caps**

Preheat oven to broil. Place chicken in a shallow pan with onion slices. Combine butter with sherry. Pour ⅓ of the sherry mixture over chicken and broil 6 inches from a low broiler flame for 20 minutes. Pour remaining sherry mixture over chicken and continue to broil until chicken is nicely browned (20 to 30 minutes longer). During the last 15 minutes of cooking, add the mushroom caps. **Serves 3 to 4.**

TARRAGON CHICKEN

An easy and elegant way to prepare chicken. Serve with Rissolé Potatoes and Pureed Carrots (see pages 110 and 101.).

2   **cloves garlic, crushed**
Juice of one lemon
1   **3¹/₂- to 4-pound roasting chicken**
1   **tablespoon chopped fresh tarragon, or
    1 teaspoon dried tarragon**
4   **slices bacon**

Preheat oven to 375° F. In a small bowl, combine garlic, lemon juice, and tarragon. Rub mixture inside chicken cavity and over skin. Lay bacon strips over top of chicken and roast until chicken is tender and drumstick wiggles easily. **Serves 4 to 6.**

YOGURT CHICKEN

1   2- to 3-pound frying chicken, cut into
     serving pieces
1   teaspoon freshly ground pepper
1/2 tablespoon grated fresh gingerroot.
1   cup (2 sticks) butter, at room
     temperature
1 1/2 pints plain yogurt

Rub chicken pieces with pepper and ginger. Cook chicken
in 1/2 cup butter over medium heat, turning often, until
chicken is browned and tender. Blend together remaining butter and yogurt. Spoon over chicken; reduce heat
and simmer until sauce is heated through. **Serves 4.**

FRUITED DUCKLING

1   4- to 5-pound duckling
2   apples, cored and quartered
6   prunes, pitted
Salt and freshly ground pepper
Orange sections

Preheat oven to 375° F. Rub duck inside and out with
salt and pepper. Place quartered apples and prunes in-

side cavity. Prick duck skin all over with the tines of a fork, making sure not to pierce the flesh. Place duck directly on oven rack, above a pan containing 2 inches of water to catch the drippings. Roast 2½ hours, or until drumstick wiggles easily. Remove fruit from cavity, quarter duck, and serve with fruit on the side, garnished with orange sections. **Serves 4 to 6.**

TURKEY ENCHILADAS

You can substitute equal amounts of cooked chicken or ground beef for the turkey.

> 2 **cups diced cooked turkey**
> 2 **cups shredded Monterey Jack or Muenster cheese**
> 4 to 5 **tablespoons green chili sauce**
> 8 to 10 **corn tortillas**
> **Sliced black olives**

Preheat oven to 350° F. Mix together turkey, 1 cup cheese, and chili sauce. Place a generous portion in the center of each tortilla and roll up lengthwise. Place tortillas in baking dish, seam side down, and top with additional cheese and olives. Bake 25 minutes. **Serves 4 to 6.**

YOGURT BARBECUED TURKEY

1   cup plain yogurt
¼   cup brown sugar, firmly packed
4   large cloves garlic, minced
3   tablespoons Worcestershire sauce
1   6-pound turkey breast

Combine yogurt, sugar, garlic, and Worcestershire sauce; pour over turkey breast, and allow to marinate overnight. Barbecue over low heat until very tender. **Serves 6.**

EASY

EXOTICS

SALT-PACKED CAPON

Many countries have variations of salt-packed roasting methods. The salt seals in juices during cooking without giving an overly salty flavor of its own. Make sure the roasting pan is not too much larger than the meat, however, or the salt will shift too much.

1   4- to 5-pound capon
2   tablespoons oyster mushrooms,
    chopped fine
10 pounds coarse sea salt

Preheat oven to 400° F. Loosen skin around breast of capon and slide mushrooms under skin. Pour 3 to 4 inches of salt into a heavy casserole or roasting pan. Place capon, breast side up, on salt and pack remaining salt around capon. Roast 1¾ hours, uncovered. To serve, break salt block and remove. **Serves 6.**

NOTE: Oyster mushrooms can be found in specialty shops.

SALT-PACKED
PRIME RIBS OF BEEF

Make sure that your roast is at least 3 ribs. Omit mushrooms, rub thoroughly with freshly ground pepper, and pack as above. Roast at 400° F 20 minutes to the pound for medium rare.

CHICKEN DEL CAMPO

A recipe that comes courtesy of relatives in Texas, where both Southern and Mexican influences come to bear on some fantastic cooking. If you like, garnish with shredded cheese and sliced black olives for a great buffet dish.

        12   corn tortillas
         2   cups diced chicken
         2   cups sour cream
    3 to 4   tablespoons paprika
             Freshly ground black pepper to taste

Preheat oven to 375° F. In a 9 by 13 by 2 baking pan, beginning with a layer of tortillas, layer the above ingredients, ending with a layer of sour cream and paprika. Bake 25 minutes, or until top layer is slightly browned and bubbly. **Serves 6.**

CHINESE SMOKED CHICKEN

This easy recipe "smokes" the chicken in foil. Experiment with your favorite teas like jasmine for some interesting flavor variations.

    2   **teaspoons whole Szechwan peppercorns, or 2 teaspoons whole black peppercorns**
    1   **2-pound chicken, cut into serving pieces**
   ¹/₂   **cup sugar**
   ¹/₂   **cup tea leaves (Lapsang Souchong is best)**
    2   **teaspoons hot sesame oil**

Preheat oven to 350° F. Grind peppercorns in a mill or place between 2 sheets of wax paper and crush with a mallet. Rub ground peppercorns into chicken pieces thoroughly, on both sides. Allow to stand several hours. Place a large sheet of aluminum foil on a baking sheet; sprinkle with tea leaves and sugar. Put a wire rack, large enough to hold chicken pieces, on the foil; place chicken pieces on the rack. Draw up the ends of the foil to make a tightly sealed tent; fold over edges to seal chicken inside. Bake for 35 minutes. Fold foil edges back; brush chicken with sesame oil. Return chicken to oven and allow to brown an additional 15 minutes. **Serves 4.**

POTTED SQUABS

2   cloves garlic, minced
$1/2$ teaspoon sage, crumbled
6   squabs, cleaned and dressed, or 6 Rock
    Cornish game hens
6   slices bacon

Preheat oven to 400° F. In a small bowl, combine garlic and sage and rub squabs with this mixture. Wrap each bird in a slice of bacon and roast, uncovered, in a pan containing $1/2$ inch of water, basting frequently, for 30 minutes. **Serves 4 to 6.**

SEAFOOD

CRAB AMANDINE

1   pound fresh lump crabmeat
$1/2$ cup butter
Juice of 1 lemon
$1^{1/2}$ tablespoons minced parsley
$3/4$ cup slivered almonds

In a medium skillet, sauté crabmeat in 2 tablespoons butter over low heat for 5 minutes. Transfer to serving platter and keep warm. Add remaining butter, lemon juice, parsley, and almonds to skillet and cook until almonds begin to brown and parsley is limp. Pour almond sauce over crab and serve. **Serves 4.**

CRAB LOUIS

Serve on lettuce leaves, garnished with plenty of tomato.

   $\frac{1}{2}$ **cup tomato-based chili sauce**
   $\frac{3}{4}$ **cup mayonnaise**
   $\frac{1}{2}$ **pound fresh lump crabmeat**
     Lemon juice, optional

In a medium bowl, combine chili sauce, mayonnaise, and crabmeat, and lemon juice if desired. Chill thoroughly. **Serves 2.**

RUSSIAN CRAB

1   cup mayonnaise
1/2   cup tomato-based chili sauce
1/2   pound fresh lump crabmeat
1   1/2-ounce can black caviar
1   hard-cooked egg yolk

Combine mayonnaise, chili sauce, and crabmeat; top with caviar. Force egg yolk through a sieve and garnish. Serve well chilled. **Serves 2.**

STEAMED MUSSELS WITH WINE

Serve with plenty of hot garlic bread.

3/4   cup chopped onion
2   cloves garlic, minced
1/4   cup butter
11/3   cup dry white wine
4   pounds mussels, washed, beards removed

In a large saucepan, sauté onion and garlic in butter until golden. Pour in wine; add mussels, and bring liquid to a boil over high heat. Reduce heat, cover, and steam mussels approximately 7 minutes, shaking pan once or twice, until shells have opened. Serve in bowls with sauce poured over. **Serves 4 to 5.**

BASTED OYSTERS

1 **pint shucked oysters**
1 **ounce slab bacon**
2 **tablespoons butter**
¼ **cup chopped scallions**
Juice of one lemon

Preheat oven to broil. Arrange oysters in a shallow pan. In a medium skillet, sauté bacon in butter until bacon is crisp. Remove bacon and discard (or eat). Add scallions and lemon juice to skillet and pour a small amount over oysters. Broil, basting occasionally with remaining sauce, until oysters begin to curl at the edges. **Serves 4.**

SCALLOPS AND BACON

20   sea scallops
10   slices bacon, cut in half
     Juice of 1 lemon
     Freshly ground pepper

Wrap each scallop in ½ slice of bacon. Thread 4 or 5 scallops onto 6-inch skewers and broil 5 minutes. To serve, squeeze lemon juice over all and garnish with freshly ground pepper. **Serves 4 to 5.**

BROILED SCALLOPS WITH SNOW PEAS

½   teaspoon dried red pepper, or to taste
½   pound snow pea pods
1   pound sea scallops
    Juice of one lemon
½   cup dry white wine

Toss red pepper with snow pea pods in an 8-inch shallow baking dish. Arrange scallops on top; add lemon juice and white wine. Broil until scallops are tender and lightly browned, about 7 minutes. **Serves 4.**

SEAFOOD TARRAGON

16   large shrimp, shelled and deveined
16   sea scallops
$^{1}/_{2}$ cup butter
 1   tablespoon fresh tarragon, or
     1 teaspoon dried tarragon
$^{1}/_{2}$ cup dry sherry

Preheat oven to 375° F. Place shrimp and scallops in a
shallow baking dish. In a medium saucepan, melt butter
over low heat; add tarragon and sherry and bring to a
boil. Simmer 2 minutes. Pour mixture over fish and bake
15 to 20 minutes. **Serves 4 to 5.**

SAUTÉED BARBECUE SHRIMP

1   cup salted butter
2   large cloves garlic, minced
1   tablespoon Italian seasoning
1   teaspoon cayenne pepper
2   pounds medium shrimp, in the shells

Preheat oven to 300° F. In a medium oven-proof skillet,
sauté butter, garlic, and seasoning. Remove from heat
and allow to stand 30 minutes or more. Wash shrimp;

dry thoroughly with a paper towel, and squeeze to remove excess moisture. Sauté shrimp in butter mixture over low heat until slightly pink and just beginning to curl. Transfer skillet to oven and bake 15 minutes. To serve, heap shrimp into bowls and top with plenty of sauce. The shells can be eaten if desired, but at any rate this dish is best eaten with the fingers. **Serves 6.**

SHRIMP AND CREAM

1	**pound large shrimp, shelled and deveined**
1/4	**cup sherry**
1	**teaspoon salt**
1/2	**cup heavy cream**
1/2	**pound Monterey Jack cheese, shredded**

Preheat oven to broil. Place shrimp in casserole dish with sherry and salt. Add cream and top with the shredded cheese. Broil until shrimp are slightly curled and pink and cheese is bubbly. **Serves 4.**

BROILED ORIENTAL SHRIMP

1   large clove garlic, minced
2   teaspoons powdered ginger
3   tablespoons peanut oil
3   tablespoons soy sauce
1½ pounds large shrimp, shelled and
     deveined

In a small bowl mix together garlic, ginger, peanut oil, and soy sauce. Place shrimp in an 8-inch shallow pan. Pour the soy sauce mixture over shrimp and marinate 1 hour. Place shrimp on broiling rack; broil 3 to 4 minutes on each side, or until pink and slightly curled. **Serves 4.**

SHRIMP SCAMPI I

¼ cup butter, melted
¼ cup olive oil
  Freshly ground pepper
½ teaspoon salt
24 large shrimp, shelled and deveined
24 large shrimp, shelled and deveined

Preheat oven to broil. Combine butter, oil, pepper, and salt in a large bowl; add shrimp and toss well to coat. Place shrimp on broiling rack; broil 3 minutes on each side. Shrimp are done when slightly curled and pale pink. **Serves 4.**

SHRIMP SCAMPI II

½   cup olive oil
Freshly ground pepper
2   cloves garlic, crushed
24   large shrimp, shelled and deveined
Freshly grated Parmesan cheese

Preheat oven to broil. Combine oil, pepper, and garlic together in a large bowl. Add shrimp and toss well to coat. Roll shrimp in freshly grated Parmesan cheese and place on a broiling rack. Broil 4 minutes on each side. **Serves 4.**

VIRGINIA SHRIMP

2   pounds shrimp, shelled
     and deveined
¾   cup butter
2   cups seasoned bread crumbs
4   cloves garlic, minced
1   cup dry sherry

Preheat oven to 350° F. Place cleaned shrimp in 2 quarts boiling water. Return water to boiling and continue cooking for 2 minutes. Drain. Melt ½ cup butter in large skillet; add garlic and sauté until garlic is lightly browned. Add bread crumbs and sherry and cook 1 minute. Remove from heat. Beginning with a layer of shrimp, place alternating layers of shrimp and bread-crumb mixture in a well-buttered 2-quart baking dish, ending with a layer of bread crumbs. Dot with remaining butter and bake 15 minutes. **Serves 4 to 6.**

FILLET OF SOLE WITH HERB BUTTER

To get the maximum flavor, combine butter with your choice of seasonings and refrigerate at least 8 hours.

Your choice of the following seasonings:
- **¼ teaspoon dried rosemary**
- **¼ teaspoon ground fennel seed**
- **1 teaspoon lemon zest**

- **4 tablespoons butter**
- **1 pound sole fillets**

Salt and pepper to taste.

Combine your choice of seasoning with softened butter. In a large skillet, melt the butter until it sizzles. Add sole fillets and sauté for 2 minutes on each side. **Serves 2 to 3.**

FILLET OF SOLE
IN TARRAGON

$1/2$	cup butter
1	small onion, chopped
$1^{1}/_{2}$	pound sole fillets
$1/2$	cup dry vermouth
2	tablespoons chopped fresh tarragon, or 2 teaspoons dried tarragon

Preheat oven to 350° F. In a small skillet over low heat melt 2 tablespoons butter; add onion, and sauté until translucent. Have ready a 25-inch piece of aluminun foil laid out on a flat surface; arrange fillets in center of foil. Cut remaining butter into $1/2$-inch pieces and place over fillets. Sprinkle with vermouth and tarragon and arrange onions over all. The edges of the foil must be securely folded to insure that minimal moisture escapes during cooking. To seal, fold one side of foil over fillets. Roll up the edges tightly so that the foil is sealed on all sides. Place foil in baking dish and bake 20 minutes. Open foil and bake 10 minutes more, allowing fish to brown. **Serves 4.**

EASY

EXOTICS

SHRIMP IN COCONUT MILK

1 **pound shrimp, shelled and deveined, shells reserved**
3 **cloves garlic, crushed**
¼ **cup lime juice**
¼ **cup butter**
1 **15-ounce can unsweetened coconut milk, or 1 cup fresh coconut milk (see page 33)**

Marinate shrimp in garlic and lime juice 1 hour. Meanwhile, in a small saucepan combine shrimp shells and 2 cups water. Bring to a boil and cook until liquid is reduced by one-half. Remove shells and discard. Melt butter until foaming; add marinade liquid, shrimp stock, and coconut milk and simmer until mixture is slightly thick. Add shrimp to the hot sauce and cook until shrimp are pink and very slightly curled, about 3 minutes. **Serves 4.**

SHRIMP EGG FOO YUNG WITH SCALLIONS

6   eggs
1/2 teaspoon salt
1/2 pound shrimp, shelled and deveined
3   scallions, chopped
5   tablespoons peanut oil

Beat eggs with salt in a small bowl. In a large skillet or wok, sauté shrimp and scallions in 2 tablespoons oil until shrimp are pink and slightly curled; with a slotted spoon, remove shrimp and scallions and set aside. Heat remaining oil very hot. Add eggs and swirl evenly to coat bottom and sides of pan. Add the shrimp and scallions, continue cooking a few moments longer. Loosen edges of egg foo yung, turn, and brown slightly on other side. **Serves 4.**

SHRIMP CAKES WITH PORK

1/2 pound shrimp, shelled and deveined
1/2 pound hot pork sausage
1/2 cup chopped scallions
1   clove garlic, minced
3   tablespoons peanut oil

Grind shrimp in work bowl of a food processor fitted with a steel knife. Add pork sausage, scallions, and garlic and process a few seconds more, until mixture is very smooth. Heat oil in a heavy skillet or wok. Form shrimp mixture into small patties, about 1½ inches in diameter, and fry until cooked through and golden brown on both sides. Sprinkle with soy sauce before serving, if desired. **Serves 6.**

CRISPY PRAWNS

Prawns are actually smaller river shrimp, but hard to find, so we have substituted jumbo shrimp in this recipe. Always, when cooking shrimp, be careful not to overcook.

16 jumbo shrimp, shelled and deveined, tails left intact
2 tablespoons gin
2 eggs, beaten
4 tablespoons cornstarch
Oil for deep frying

Butterfly the shrimp by cutting a deep slit along back curve, almost to inner edge; open and flatten slightly, using bottom of a cup or flat side of a knife. Place in a shallow pan; pour gin over and allow to stand 15 minutes. Dip each shrimp in egg, then in cornstarch to coat. Heat oil to 350° F. Fry shrimp, a few at a time, until golden brown and crisp, about 3 minutes. **Serves 4 to 6.**

POACHED TROUT WITH WALNUT SAUCE

2   cups shelled walnuts
1/2 teaspoon salt
1/2 cup water
1/4 cup red wine vinegar
6   fresh trout, cleaned, heads removed

In work bowl of food processor or blender, grind walnuts and salt together until they form a thick paste. Combine water and vinegar. Pour liquid through feed tube in a thin stream until mixture is blended and smooth. Place fish in a large skillet with enough boiling water to just barely cover. Season water with chopped parsley and a few whole peppercorns, if desired. Simmer, covered, until fish is easily flaked with a fork but still moist, about 10 minutes. To serve, transfer fish to a heated platter, season with salt to taste, and top with walnut sauce. Serve warm or chilled. **Serves 4 to 6.**

The Vegetable Express

All of the following recipes, with the exception of Chilled Dilled Peas, call for fresh vegetables. Since fresh produce is available in nearly all parts of the country year round, we prefer to use them whenever possible. Should you wish to substitute frozen vegetables, we suggest steaming instead of boiling as a cooking method, since most commercially prepared vegetables have been precooked. In fact, we prefer steaming fresh vegetables too whenever possible, because, even though it takes a little longer than boiling, the results are worth the effort in color, texture, and nutritional value.

Many of these recipes can be served as a main course instead of a more traditional side dish. Leeks in Pastry, Potato Pancakes, or Stuffed Eggplant accompanied by a salad or soup would make a great lunch or supper.

Leftover vegetables make fine additions to soups and stews, so be creative and don't hesitate to experiment.

ASPARAGUS WITH CHEESE SAUCE

1   pound asparagus, washed and trimmed
1   tablespoon butter
1   tablespoon all-purpose flour
¹/₂   cup half and half
³/₄   cup grated cheese (American or any mild cheddar)

Steam asparagus over boiling water until tender, approximately 15 minutes, depending on the size of the spears. Meanwhile, melt butter in a medium saucepan over low heat. Add flour and stir to make a roux; cook 2 to 3 minutes. Gradually add cream, beating continuously with a wire whisk until sauce is smooth and slightly thickened. Add cheese and whisk until melted. To serve, arrange steamed asparagus on serving dish; pour sauce over and serve immediately. **Serves 4.**

ASPARAGUS WITH PROSCIUTTO

³/₄   **pound fresh asparagus spears, washed and trimmed**
¹/₄   **pound prosciutto, thinly sliced**
¹/₄   **cup butter, melted**
2   **tablespoons grated Parmesan cheese**

Preheat oven to broil. Steam asparagus spears just until tender; do not overcook. Wrap 2 or 3 spears in 1 slice of prosciutto and place seam side down in a shallow pan. Pour melted butter over asparagus bundles and top with cheese. Place under broiler until cheese is lightly toasted, about 3 minutes. **Serves 4.**

GUACAMOLE

1   **ripe medium avocado, peeled, pitted, and mashed**
1   **tablespoon mayonnaise**
¹/₂   **medium tomato, finely chopped**
2   **tablespoons grated onion**
Tabasco sauce to taste

Combine all ingredients by hand or whirl for a few seconds in work bowl of food processor or blender. Serve immediately as a dip or on lettuce leaves as a salad.

NOTE: If guacamole is to be kept for more than an hour, add juice of 1 lemon to retain color and store in refrigerator.

GREEN BEANS AMANDINE

1   pound green beans, washed and trimmed
1/3   cup butter
1/2   cup sliced almonds
   Salt and pepper to taste

Steam green beans over boiling water until tender yet crisp. Remove from heat. Melt butter in a large skillet; add almonds and sauté until lightly browned. Remove almonds from pan; add beans and sauté until heated through. Season with salt and pepper. Transfer green beans to serving platter and garnish with sautéed almonds. **Serves 4 to 6.**

GREEN BEANS AND GARLIC

2   cloves garlic, crushed
3   tablespoons peanut oil
1   pound green beans, washed, trimmed, and cut into 2-inch pieces
3   tablespoons soy sauce
1 1/2   teaspoons sugar

In a large skillet, sauté garlic in oil until lightly browned. Remove garlic and discard. Add green beans and stir fry over high heat until tender yet still crisp. Add soy sauce and sugar, blending well. Continue to cook until heated through. **Serves 4.**

SWEET AND SOUR BEETS

1 **pound beets, washed, trimmed, and cut into ¼-inch slices**
2 **teaspoons sugar**
¼ **cup cider vinegar**
2 **teaspoons cornstarch**
½ **cup butter**

Place beets in a saucepan with enough water to cover. Bring to a boil, cover, and cook beets until tender, 12 to 15 minutes. Meanwhile, in a small saucepan, dissolve sugar in vinegar and heat just to boiling. In a small bowl, combine cornstarch with a little water to make a paste. Add 2 tablespoons heated sugar mixture to cornstarch and blend. Pour cornstarch mixture into sugar mixture, stirring constantly over low heat until slightly thickened. Add butter, a little at a time, stirring until melted. To serve, arrange drained beets on serving dish and pour sauce over. Serve hot or cold. **Serves 4 to 6.**

(NOTE: If you prefer a thinner sauce, add a little beet water.)

BROCCOLI WITH GARLIC AND SESAME

1 large bunch broccoli, washed, trimmed, and broken into florets
2 cloves garlic, crushed
3 tablespoons sesame oil
Fresh lemon juice

In a large pot, steam broccoli over boiling water until tender yet still crisp. In a large skillet, sauté garlic in oil until brown. Discard garlic. Add broccoli to skillet and cook over moderate heat 3 to 4 minutes, stirring occasionally. Serve with a squeeze of fresh lemon juice. **Serves 4.**

BROCCOLI PUREE

1 bunch broccoli, about 1½ pounds, washed, trimmed, and broken into florets
3 tablespoons butter
1 large clove garlic, minced
¼ cup half and half or light cream
2 heaping tablespoons grated Parmesan cheese

Place broccoli in a medium saucepan and cover with cold water. Bring to a boil, reduce heat, and simmer 15 minutes or until very tender; drain. Place broccoli in work bowl of food processor fitted with a steel knife; puree. Add butter, garlic, half and half, and cheese and whirl for a few seconds more. Return puree to saucepan and heat over a low flame until hot. **Serves 4.**

SESAME BROCCOLI

1   **large bunch broccoli, washed, trimmed, and broken into florets**
¹/₂ **cup sesame seeds, toasted**
1¹/₂ **tablespoons soy sauce**
2   **tablespoons hot sesame oil**
2   **teaspoons honey**

Steam broccoli over boiling water until tender; set aside to cool. Combine sesame seeds, soy sauce, oil, and honey, reserving ¹/₄ cup sesame seeds for garnish. To serve, arrange broccoli on serving platter, pour dressing over, and sprinkle with remaining seeds. Serve at room temperature or chilled. **Serves 4.**

BRUSSELS SPROUTS WITH CURRIED CREAM

1½ pounds Brussels sprouts, washed and trimmed

CURRIED CREAM:
1½ cups sour cream
½ cup mayonnaise
1 tablespoon curry powder, or to taste
1 large clove garlic, crushed

Steam Brussels sprouts over boiling water until tender, 7 to 10 minutes. Chill. In a medium serving bowl, blend together sour cream, mayonnaise, curry powder, and garlic. Place colored toothpicks in chilled sprouts and arrange around curried cream. **Serves 6.**

SWEET AND SOUR CABBAGE

1 tablespoon vegetable oil
½ teaspoon red pepper flakes
5 tablespoons sugar
½ cup white vinegar
1 pound cabbage, cut into bite-sized pieces

Heat oil, pepper, sugar, and vinegar together in a small saucepan. Place cabbage in a large container that can be tightly covered. Pour heated dressing over cabbage; allow to cool, then cover tightly. Store in refrigerator overnight to marinate before serving. **Makes approximately 1 quart.**

MAPLE CARROTS

6   **large carrots, washed, trimmed, and cut into ¼-inch rounds**

2   **medium apples, peeled, cored, and sliced**

3   **tablespoons maple syrup**

2   **tablespoons brown sugar**

2½   **tablespoons butter, cut into pieces**

Preheat oven to 375° F. Steam carrots over boiling water until tender yet still crisp. Place apples in an 8-inch shallow baking dish; top with sliced carrots. Combine syrup and sugar and pour over carrots. Dot with butter and bake until bubbly. **Serves 4.**

PUREED CARROTS

- 2 pounds carrots, washed, trimmed, and cut into 1/4-inch rounds
- 1/2 teaspoon salt
- 6 tablespoons sweet butter, cut into 1/4-inch cubes
- 1 1/2 teaspoons ground ginger
- 1/4 cup half and half, heated

Place carrots in a saucepan with salt and enough water to cover; bring to a boil, then reduce heat and cook until tender, about 20 minutes. Drain carrots and place in work bowl of food processor fitted with a steel knife, or in a blender. Add butter and ginger and process until smooth. Gradually add half and half, and process 1 minute longer. Serve immediately, or place in top half of double boiler over hot water to keep warm. **Serves 6.**

CURRIED CAULIFLOWER

- 1 small head cauliflower, washed, trimmed, and broken into florets
- 4 tablespoons butter
- 1 teaspoon lemon juice
- 2 teaspoons curry powder
- 1/2 teaspoon salt

Steam cauliflower over boiling water until tender. Meanwhile, melt butter in a small saucepan; add lemon juice, curry powder, and salt and cook over low heat until bubbly. Pour over cauliflower and serve. **Serves 4.**

CREAMED CORN

1   **tablespoon butter**
2   **cups fresh corn, cut from 4 to 6 cobs.**
3   **tablespoons heavy cream**
1   **tablespoon water**
A pinch of ground cloves

Melt butter in medium saucepan over moderate heat; add corn, cover, and cook until tender. Add cream, water, and cloves and simmer until corn is very soft and sauce is creamy, about 5 minutes. **Serves 4.**

CUCUMBERS IN SOUR CREAM

2   **medium cucumbers, thinly sliced**
1   **cup sour cream**
1   **bunch scallions, washed, trimmed, and chopped**
1   **tablespoon white vinegar**
1   **teaspoon sugar**

Rinse cucumber slices in cold water and dry thoroughly. Place in medium bowl; add sour cream, scallions, vinegar, and sugar and mix well. Marinate in refrigerator 2 to 3 hours before serving. **Serves 4.**

EGGPLANT BUTTER

- 1 **pound eggplant, peeled and cut into 1-inch pieces**
- 2 **tablespoons tahini (sesame paste), or 2 tablespoons chunky peanut butter**
- 1 **large clove garlic, crushed**
- 2 **teaspoons hot sesame oil**
- 1 **teaspoon salt**

Steam eggplant over boiling water until very soft. Combine with tahini, garlic, oil, and salt by hand, or whirl for a few seconds in work bowl of food processor or blender until smooth. Can be used as a vegetable side dish, a sandwich filling, or a dip. **Makes about 2 cups.**

MEDITERRANEAN EGGPLANT

- 1 **medium eggplant**
- 1 **large clove garlic, crushed**
- ¹/₂ **cup olive oil**
- 1 **teaspoon capers**
- 1 **teaspoon dry mustard**

Roast unpeeled eggplant directly over a low flame on stove burner or in a 375° F oven, until skin appears charred and eggplant collapses. Remove from heat and cool. Scoop out pulp and place in work bowl of food processor fitted with a steel knife or in a blender. Add garlic, oil, capers, and mustard and process a few seconds until well blended. Serve at room temperature or chilled. **Serves 4.**

STUFFED EGGPLANT

1   **large eggplant, approximately 1 pound**
2   **onions, chopped**
3   **large cloves garlic, crushed**
Freshly ground pepper
Grated Parmesan cheese or bread crumbs, if desired

Preheat oven to 350° F. Halve eggplant lengthwise. Scoop out pulp, leaving the shell intact. Dice eggplant pulp and combine with onions, garlic, and pepper. Sauté in a large saucepan over moderate heat for 5 minutes. Stuff mixture into shells and sprinkle with Parmesan cheese or bread crumbs, if desired. Bake 25 minutes. Serve hot or cold. **Serves 4 to 6.**

EGGPLANT AND YOGURT SALAD

1 large eggplant, peeled and cut into
1-inch chunks
¼ cup olive oil
1 large red onion, chopped
3 medium tomatoes, chopped
1 cup plain yogurt

Steam eggplant over boiling water until soft. Combine with onion, tomatoes, and yogurt. Chill thoroughly before serving. **Serves 4.**

LEEKS IN PASTRY

1 17½-ounce package frozen puff pastry
1 pound leeks, washed, trimmed, and
diced
¾ cup butter
½ cup sour cream
1 egg yolk

Preheat oven to 425° F. Thaw pastry and roll out edges. Fit one sheet of pastry into a 9-inch pie plate. Over moderate heat, sauté leeks in half the butter until liquid is absorbed. Add sour cream and blend. Pour leek mixture into crust; cut remaining butter into ¹/₂-inch cubes and place on top of leek mixture. Cover with second sheet of pastry, crimping edges together to seal tightly. Brush pastry with egg yolk, and prick with a toothpick or skewer to allow steam to escape during baking. Place in oven and bake 10 minutes. Reduce heat to 375° F and bake an additional 45 minutes or until pastry is puffed and golden. This dish makes an excellent first course or main dish. **Serves 4 to 6.**

CURRIED ONIONS

The very slow cooking of the onions in this recipe gives them a very delicate, almost sweet taste. Delicious!

    4   **medium white onions, thinly sliced**
    ¹/₂ **cup butter**
    2   **teaspoons curry powder**
        Salt and pepper to taste

Sauté onions in butter over very low heat until limp and translucent. Stir in curry powder and salt and pepper and continue cooking another 3 to 4 minutes. **Serves 4.**

CHILLED DILLED PEAS

1 teaspoon curry powder, or to taste
1 cup sour cream
1/2 cup fresh snipped chives
1/4 cup fresh snipped dill
1 16-ounce can tiny peas, drained and
   rinsed in cold water, or 1 10-ounce box
   frozen tiny peas, cooked and drained

Combine curry powder, sour cream, chives, and dill;
add peas and mix gently, but thoroughly. Garnish with
additional fresh dill, if desired, and chill. This dish makes
an excellent first course, vegetable side dish, or appetizer. **Serves 4 to 6.**

SNOW PEA PODS
WITH MUSHROOMS

3/4 pound snow pea pods, washed, ends
    trimmed
1/2 pound fresh mushrooms, sliced
3   scallions, chopped
1/4 cup butter

Sauté vegetables in butter over medium high heat until
crisp tender. **Serves 4.**

BAKED POTATO CHIPS

3   pounds white boiling potatoes, cut
    crosswise into 1/8-inch slices
4   tablespoons butter, melted
Salt and pepper to taste

Preheat oven to 500° F. Lightly grease 2 baking sheets.
Place potato slices in a single layer on baking sheets and
brush generously with butter. Bake 15 minutes or until
potatoes are crisp and browned around the edges.
Transfer to a heated platter and season with salt and
pepper. **Serves 4.**

NEW POTATOES
WITH ROSEMARY

1   pound small new potatoes (red skinned
    are best)
2   teaspoons salt
1   tablespoon crumbled rosemary
2   tablespoons butter
Salt and pepper to taste

In a large saucepan, combine potatoes and enough water
to cover. Bring water to a boil; add salt and simmer,
covered, 15 to 20 minutes. Drain potatoes. Return po-

tatoes to pan; turn heat to low, cover, and cook, shaking pan occasionally, about 2 minutes longer, or until all moisture has evaporated. Add rosemary and butter and toss lightly. Season to taste with salt and pepper. **Serves 4.**

POTATO PANCAKES

3   **large potatoes, peeled and cut into large chunks**
1   **medium onion, minced**
2   **eggs, lightly beaten**
2   **tablespoons all-purpose flour**
¹/₂ **cup vegetable oil**

Place potatoes in work bowl of food processor fitted with a steel knife. Process a few seconds, or until potatoes are consistency of chunky applesauce. Add onion, eggs, and flour and process for a few more seconds. Heat ¹/₄ cup of oil in a large skillet. Use approximately 2 tablespoons mixture for each pancake and fry 5 to 7 minutes on each side until the outside is golden brown and crisp. Drain on absorbent paper. Add more oil as necessary for frying the remaining mixture. Serve with applesauce or sour cream. **Serves 4.**

RISSOLÉ POTATOES

2   pounds boiling potatoes
1/4   cup butter
2   tablespoons chopped fresh parsley
Salt and pepper to taste

Peel potatoes and cover with cold water to prevent discoloration. Cut small balls out of potatoes with a melon-
ball cutter. Drop potato balls into boiling salted water
and cook covered, 7 to 8 minutes. Do not overcook.
Drain potato balls and pat dry. Heat butter in a medium
skillet; when sizzling, add potato balls and cook until
golden brown on all sides. Add chopped fresh parsley
and cook 1 minute more. Season with salt and pepper
to taste. **Serves 4 to 6.**

YOGURT POTATOES

8   new potatoes
2   scallions, chopped
1/4   cup plain yogurt
1 1/2   teaspoons milk
Chopped fresh parsley

Scrub potatoes thoroughly; do not peel. Cook in salted water to cover 15 to 20 minutes, or until tender. Drain. Combine chopped scallions, yogurt, and milk. Add potatoes and toss lightly. Top with parsley and serve hot. **Serves 6 to 8.**

NO-CRUST
SPINACH QUICHE

Butter
4   ounces shredded mild cheddar cheese, about 1 cup
3   tablespoons minced onion
6   eggs
1½   pounds fresh spinach, washed, trimmed, and dried, or 2 10-ounce packages frozen chopped spinach, cooked and drained

Preheat oven to 400° F. Generously butter a shallow baking dish. In a medium bowl, toss together ¾ cup of the cheese and minced onion; spread over bottom of dish. In the same bowl, beat eggs lightly; add spinach and toss well. Spread spinach-egg mixture evenly over cheese-onion mixture, and top with remaining cheese. Bake 20 minutes, or until cheese is browned and bubbly. **Serves 6.**

SPINACH WITH SESAME SEEDS

1   **pound fresh spinach, well rinsed in cold water, stems removed**
1   **tablespoon sesame seeds, toasted**
1/2   **teaspoon sesame oil**
Salt and pepper, if desired

Steam spinach over boiling water until tender. Transfer to a small bowl, add sesame seeds and oil, and toss lightly. Season with salt and pepper. **Serves 4.**

SPINACH WITH SOUR CREAM

1   **pound fresh spinach, washed, trimmed, and dried**
1/4   **cup butter, melted**
1/2   **cup sour cream**
1/2   **cup grated Romano cheese**
Freshly ground pepper

Preheat oven to broil. Sauté spinach in butter until limp; squeeze out excess moisture. Transfer to a 1-quart baking dish; add sour cream and 1/4 cup cheese and mix well. Top with remaining cheese and freshly ground pepper and place under broiler until cheese is lightly browned, about 3 minutes. **Serves 4.**

SPINACH WITH WALNUTS

1 **pound fresh spinach, washed, trimmed, and dried**
3/4 **cup sour cream**
1/2 **cup walnuts, finely chopped**
3 **scallions, finely chopped**

Preheat oven to 325° F. Mix spinach, sour cream, walnuts, and scallions together in a well-buttered 1½-quart baking dish, and bake at 325° F for 25 minutes. **Serves 4.**

TOMATO AND MOZZARELLA SALAD

2 **large ripe tomatoes, each cut into eight wedges**
8 **ounces full-cream mozzarella, cut into 1/2-inch cubes**
1 **bunch fresh basil, washed, trimmed, and chopped**
1/2 **cup olive oil**
3 **tablespoons red wine vinegar**

Place tomatoes, cheese, and basil in serving bowl. In a separate container, shake the oil and vinegar together until well blended and pour over salad, tossing ingredients to mix. Marinate in refrigerator at least 2 hours before serving. **Serves 4.**

ZUCCHINI BROIL

1/4 **cup butter**
  2 **medium zucchini, washed and thinly sliced**
  2 **medium tomatoes, sliced**
  2 **cloves garlic, crushed**
  1 **cup shredded mozzarella cheese**

Preheat oven to broil. Melt butter in a medium oven-proof skillet; add zucchini, tomatoes, and garlic and cook, stirring occasionally, over moderate heat 10 to 15 minutes, or until zucchini is just tender. Sprinkle with cheese and place under the broiler until cheese is melted and bubbly. **Serves 4.**

ZUCCHINI ROQUEFORT

4 **medium zucchini, washed and trimmed**
¹/₂ **cup Roquefort salad dressing**
¹/₂ **cup cornflakes, crumbled**
¹/₄ **cup olive oil**

Cut zucchini into ¹/₂-inch slices. Dip each slice in salad dressing, then roll in crumbs to coat. Heat oil in a medium skillet; add zucchini slices. Fry over moderate heat until tender and golden brown, turning once. **Serves 4.**

EGGPLANT ROQUEFORT

Proceed as for above recipe, substituting 1 pound peeled, sliced eggplant for zucchini.

SPANAKOPITTA

Spinach in phyllo leaves.

2   **pounds fresh spinach, washed, trimmed, dried, and finely chopped**

¼   **cup chopped onion**

1   **16-ounce package phyllo leaves or strudel dough (if frozen, place in refrigerator overnight to defrost)**

½   **cup butter, melted**

1   **pound Gruyère cheese, grated**

Preheat oven to 350° F. Generously butter a 9 by 13 by 2 pan. In a medium bowl, combine spinach with chopped onion. Stack phyllo on work surface; cover with waxed paper and damp towel to prevent drying. Remove top sheet of phyllo and place in buttered pan; brush with melted butter. Spread a thin layer of spinach-onion mixture over phyllo. Layer the next sheet of phyllo in pan; brush with melted butter. Sprinkle a thin layer of cheese evenly over phyllo sheet. Proceed with layering, using above technique, until all of spinach mixture and cheese have been used. Butter each remaining sheet of phyllo and place over top, folding ends under as necessary to fit the pan. Brush top with butter. Make 5 or 6 slits through top of pastry with sharp knife, to allow steam to escape during baking. Bake until golden and crisp, about 40 minutes. **Serves 6 to 8.**

SPANISH SPINACH

1   pound fresh spinach, washed and
    trimmed, or 1 10-ounce package frozen
    spinach, defrosted and excess
    moisture squeezed out
1   teaspoon olive oil
1/4 cup pine nuts
1/4 cup golden raisins
    Salt to taste

Sauté spinach in olive oil over medium heat until wilted.
Remove from heat; add remaining ingredients and mix
well. **Serves 4.**

TOFU WITH SOY SAUCE

To the uninitiated, tofu (bean curd) has an unfamiliar texture and that is the reason many people object to it. Freezing tofu, however, changes the texture so that it loses its slightly spongy quality and becomes more the texture of cooked chicken or turkey.

> 3 **tablespoons sesame oil**
> 6 **cakes tofu, cut into 2-inch chunks (freeze first, if desired)**
> 2 **tablespoons soy sauce**
> 1 **scallion, minced**
> ½ **cup chicken stock, homemade or canned**

Heat sesame oil very hot; add tofu and stir fry until lightly browned. Add soy sauce and scallion and stir fry a few seconds more. Add stock, cover, and steam 5 minutes. Serve hot. **Serves 4.**

Pasta, Rice, and Cheese

PASTA

FRESH PASTA

2 cups flour
4 eggs
¹/₂ teaspoon salt
1 tablespoon olive oil

Mound flour on a clean work surface. Make a well in the center; break eggs into well and add salt and oil. Beat eggs with a fork 1 minute. Gradually mix flour into eggs with fingertips, moving hand in circular motion, until mixture forms a crumbly paste. Shape dough into a ball with hands or dough scraper. The dough should be very soft. Scrape off caked flour from board. Wash and dry hands. Lightly flour clean surface and knead dough, adding only enough additional flour to prevent sticking, until smooth and elastic, 8 to 10 minutes. (To test if dough is ready, stick finger into center of dough. Dough should feel slightly sticky but not wet; if wet, add a little more flour and continue to knead.) Wrap dough in plastic wrap dusted lightly with flour. Let rest at room temperature 1 hour.

To roll out dough, flatten on lightly floured surface that is at least 24 by 24 inches. Roll quickly away from the body. Flour the rolling pin and roll it over the dough so that you roll from the center to the edges. Turn dough 90° and roll again. Keep rolling this way until you reach desired thickness, about ⅛ inch. If at any time the dough begins to stick, lift it carefully and sprinkle more flour under it.

To make fettuccine, cut dough into strips ¼ inch wide and 10 inches long.

WHOLE-WHEAT PASTA

Substitute 1 cup whole-wheat flour for 1 cup of all-purpose flour, and proceed as above.

SPINACH PASTA

Add ¼ cup spinach puree to beaten eggs, increasing flour to 2½ cups.

NOTE: It's always a good idea to add 2 tablespoons olive oil to the water in which pasta is being cooked. It keeps it from sticking together.

FETTUCCINE ALFREDO

3 tablespoons butter
1 tablespoon flour
1/2 cup heavy cream
1/2 cup grated fresh Parmesan cheese
12 ounces fettuccine noodles, cooked and drained

Melt butter in medium saucepan over low heat. When butter begins to sizzle, add flour and stir 3 to 4 minutes. Slowly add cream and whisk together until smooth. When sauce is heated through, add Parmesan cheese and cook, stirring constantly, until cheese is melted. Season with salt and pepper if desired. Pour sauce over noodles and garnish with additional cheese. This dish is great with a little diced cooked ham or crumbled bacon. **Serves 6 as a side dish or 4 as a main course.**

FETTUCCINE WITH SMOKED SALMON

4 cups heavy cream
1/2 pound smoked salmon, cut in julienne strips
1/4 cup minced fresh dill or chives
Freshly ground pepper to taste
1 pound fettuccine noodles, cooked and drained

In a medium saucepan reduce cream over medium high heat until reduced by half. Add salmon, dill, and pepper and cook 1 minute longer. Pour over fettuccine and toss to blend. **Serves 4 as a main course.**

GERMAN NOODLES

1 medium onion, chopped
1/2 cup butter
8 ounces broad egg noodles, cooked and drained
1 8-ounce can sauerkraut, drained
Caraway seeds

In a large skillet, sauté onion in butter over medium heat until golden. Add cooked noodles and sauerkraut and toss to blend. Continue heating until very hot. Remove from heat and sprinkle with caraway seeds. Season with salt and pepper if desired. **Serves 4 as a side dish.**

GNOCCHI

Using a basic pâte à chou, gnocchi are essentially dumplings. They're excellent served with melted butter and Parmesan cheese.

½ **cup butter**
1 **cup water**
1 **cup flour**
4 **eggs**
Pinch of nutmeg

In a medium saucepan, heat butter and water together until butter melts and water begins to boil. Add the flour all at once and stir with a wooden spoon until blended. Continue cooking and stirring until mixture forms a ball and leaves the sides of the pan. Remove from heat and add eggs, one at a time, beating well after each addition. Bring 6 quarts of water to a boil; cook gnocchi by dropping half-teaspoonfuls in boiling water and poaching 3 to 4 minutes. Drain. **Serves 6 as a side dish.**

LINGUINE WITH BASIL AND PARSLEY

1 **cup olive oil**
2 **tablespoons unsalted butter**
½ **cup minced fresh basil**
½ **cup minced fresh parsley**
1 **pound linguine, cooked and drained**

Combine oil and butter in a medium skillet over moderate heat. Add basil and parsley and sauté 2 to 3 minutes. Add linguine and toss well. Serve with grated Parmesan cheese. **Serves 4.**

LINGUINE WITH WHITE CLAM SAUCE

1/2 cup butter
2 cloves garlic, minced
2 6½-ounce cans minced clams, undrained
2 tablespoons chopped parsley
1 pound linguine, cooked and drained

In a medium saucepan melt butter, add garlic, and sauté 3 to 4 minutes, or until garlic is golden. Add undrained clams and parsley and cook just until clams are heated through. Divide linguine into serving bowls, and pour clam sauce over to serve. **Serves 6 to 8 as a first course, 4 as a main course.**

LINGUINE WITH PROSCIUTTO AND MUSHROOMS

1 tablespoon butter
1/2 cup julienned prosciutto
1/2 cup sliced mushrooms
2 cups heavy cream
1 pound linguine, cooked and drained

Melt butter in medium skillet over moderate heat. Add prosciutto and mushrooms and sauté 4 to 5 minutes. Add cream and bring to a boil; boil until sauce is reduced by half. Add linguine and toss well. **Serves 4.**

NOODLE KUGEL

1   **cup cottage cheese**
1   **cup sour cream**
4   **eggs**
1   **pound wide egg noodles, cooked and drained**
Butter

Preheat oven to 350° F. In a large mixing bowl, beat cottage cheese, sour cream, and eggs together until well combined. Add noodles and toss well. Transfer to a buttered 8- or 9-inch casserole; dot with additional butter and bake until top is golden brown, about 40 minutes. **Serves 4 to 6.**

COLD NOODLES WITH SESAME SAUCE

This recipe can be made with almost any variety of noodles, from linguine to Chinese cellophane noodles. We find it particularly good with green noodles or fettuccine.

> 2   **cloves garlic, minced**
> 1   **tablespoon shredded fresh gingerroot**
> 4   **tablespoons tahini (sesame paste)**
> 2   **tablespoons soy sauce**
> 2   **teaspoons sugar, optional**
> 1   **pound noodles, cooked and drained**

In a small saucepan, heat garlic, ginger, and tahini together over moderate heat until garlic and ginger begin to brown. Add soy sauce and sugar and heat 2 minutes more. Toss with cooked noodles and serve at room temperature, or chilled, as you prefer. **Serves 4.**

NOTE: Some brands of tahini paste contain more oil than others. If the sauce seems too thick, add 1 or 2 tablespoons sesame or peanut oil to thin to desired consistency.

PASTA WITH GARLIC AND OIL

Perhaps the easiest of all pasta recipes, and one of the best. Made with fresh pasta, if can really be a delight as a side dish, or even a main course.

Toss 1 pound cooked pasta with 1 cup warm olive oil, 4 crushed cloves garlic, and 3/4 cup grated Parmesan or Romano cheese. **Serves 6 as a side dish.**

PASTA AND MORE

4 tablespoons butter
1 clove garlic, minced
1/2 cup zucchini, cut into 1/4- by 1 1/2-inch pieces
1/4 pound prosciutto, cut into 1/4- by 1 1/2-inch pieces
12 ounces green noodles, cooked and drained

Melt butter in a medium skillet over moderate heat; add garlic and zucchini, and sauté until garlic is lightly browned. Add prosciutto and cook 3 to 4 minutes longer. Remove from heat; add noodles and toss gently. Serve with Parmesan cheese, if desired. **Serves 6 as a side dish.**

PASTA CON POLLO

¹/₄ cup butter
1 tablespoon all-purpose flour
¹/₂ cup heavy cream
1¹/₂ cups diced cooked chicken
2 tablespoons sherry, optional
12 ounces spaghetti or linguine, cooked and drained

In a medium saucepan, melt butter. Add flour to make a roux and cook 2 to 3 minutes. Gradually add cream, whisking until sauce is smooth. Add chicken, and sherry if desired, and continue cooking 2 to 3 minutes. Pour sauce over pasta to serve. **Serves 4.**

For some interesting variations to the above recipe add your choice of the following ingredients:

¹/₂ teaspoon cayenne pepper
¹/₂ pound fresh, cooked mushrooms
¹/₂ cup grated Parmesan cheese

PASTA WITH RICOTTA, SPINACH, AND CREAM

2   cups heavy cream
1/4   cup cooked spinach, squeezed to
      remove excess water
3/4   cups ricotta cheese
8   ounces tubular pasta (such as penne or
      ziti), slightly undercooked
Parmesan cheese

Combine cream, spinach, and ricotta in medium sauce-pan and bring to a boil. Add pasta; toss together and continue cooking until sauce thickens slightly. Spoon into bowls and sprinkle with grated cheese. **Serves 4.**

PASTA WITH DRIED TOMATOES

12   ounces pasta, cooked and drained
1/4 pound sun-dried tomatoes in olive oil
     (available in food and specialty shops)
1   2-ounce can anchovies, drained
1   4-ounce jar pimientos
2   cloves garlic, crushed

In a medium saucepan, toss pasta with tomatoes, anchovies, pimientos, and garlic over low heat until heated through. **Serves 4.**

PASTA WITH TUNA AND FRESH BASIL

Don't hesitate to heap on plenty of Parmesan cheese before serving.

- 1   7½-ounce can tuna, packed in oil, undrained
- 4   cups cooked ziti (about 1 pound)
- ½   cup diced sweet red pepper
- ¼   cup chopped fresh basil
  Lemon juice to taste

Combine all ingredients together in a medium bowl and toss well. Chill at least 1 hour before serving. **Serves 4 as a main course.**

UNUSUAL PASTA

- 6   slices bacon, cut into 1-inch pieces
- ½   pound fresh mushrooms, sliced
- 1   cup pitted black olives
- 1   2-ounce can caper-stuffed anchovies
- 1   pound spinach fettuccine, cooked and drained

In a medium skillet, cook bacon until crisp; drain on paper towels. Pour off all but 2 tablespoons fat from skillet; add mushrooms and sauté 4 to 5 minutes. Add olives and anchovies and heat through. Toss bacon and skillet ingredients with cooked pasta and serve. **Serves 8.**

NOTE: May be additionally seasoned with Parmesan cheese, crushed red pepper, and chopped parsley, if desired.

SHELLS WITH RICOTTA CHEESE STUFFING

Pass plenty of Parmesan cheese on the side.

- 1   **pound ricotta cheese**
- ¼   **cup diced prosciutto, cooked ground veal, or spinach**
- 1   **egg, lightly beaten**
- 1   **16-ounce box large shells, cooked**
- 2   **cups hot tomato or béchamel sauce (see page 145)**

Preheat oven to 350° F. Beat ricotta, prosciutto, and egg together in a large bowl. Stuff approximately 2 tablespoons of the cheese mixture into each shell and place in a baking pan large enough to hold the shells. (A baking sheet works well, too.) Cover with aluminum foil and bake 15 to 20 minutes. Arrange shells on serving plates and pour hot sauce over. **Serves 4 to 6 as a main course.**

STUFFED SHELLS WITH THREE CHEESES

1   **pound ricotta cheese**
8   **ounces mozzarella cheese, grated**
1   **cup grated Parmesan cheese**
¼   **cup minced parsley, optional**
1   **16-ounce box large pasta shells, cooked and drained**
2   **cups tomato sauce**

Preheat oven to 350° F. In a medium bowl, mix together the cheeses, and parsley if desired, reserving ½ cup Parmesan cheese for topping. Stuff each shell with approximately 2 tablespoons cheese mixture and place in a 9 by 13 by 2 baking pan. Pour tomato sauce over and top with reserved Parmesan cheese. Bake 25 minutes or until sauce is bubbly. **Serves 4 to 6.**

TORTELLINI IN BRODO

2　quarts chicken broth
1　pound tortellini (available in food and specialty shops)
1　clove garlic, mashed
Chopped fresh parsley for garnish

Bring the broth to a boil; add tortellini and simmer until tortellini are tender, about 7 minutes. Ladle into bowls and top with parsley. **Serves 6.**

RICE

MEXICAN RICE AND CHEESE CASSEROLE

3　cups sour cream
2　4-ounce cans diced green chili peppers
Worcestershire sauce to taste
4　cups long-grain rice, cooked
1¼　pounds sharp cheddar cheese, grated

Preheat oven to 350° F. Combine all ingredients thoroughly, reserving ½ cup cheese for topping. Place in an 8- or 9-inch casserole and bake until cheese is browned and bubbly. **Serves 5.**

RICE-STUFFED PEPPERS

4	large green peppers, stems and seeds removed
1	medium onion, minced
2	cups cooked rice
½	pound ground ham or cooked pork sausage
½	teaspoon cayenne pepper, optional
1	cup shredded cheddar cheese

Preheat oven to 350° F. Parboil peppers in boiling water 5 minutes and drain. In a medium bowl, thoroughly mix onion, rice, ham, cayenne if desired, and ½ cup cheese. Stuff pepper shells generously with rice mixture and top with additional cheese. Bake at 350° F for 40 minutes, or until cheese is melted and browned. **Makes 4 peppers.**

RED RICE

1 **medium onion, minced**

3 **slices bacon**

4 **cups chopped canned tomatoes, including liquid**

1 **cup long-grain rice**

1 **teaspoon thyme**

In a medium skillet, fry bacon until crisp; drain on absorbent paper, crumble, and set aside. In fat remaining in skillet, sauté onion until golden. Add tomatoes and bring mixture to a boil. Add rice, stirring once, cover, and cook over low heat about 30 minutes, or until liquid is absorbed and rice is tender. Season with thyme. Transfer to serving dish and garnish with crumbled bacon. **Makes 6 servings.**

There is an old Creole variation of the above recipe that substitutes ½ pound chicken livers for the bacon. Cut chicken livers in half. Sauté in butter until pink, about 8 minutes, and proceed as above. The result? Something called Dirty Rice.

SPANISH RICE

Turn this side dish into a main dish, if you prefer. Transfer rice mixture to a casserole dish; top with 1 cup shredded cheddar and place under broiler 2 to 3 minutes. Serve with a green salad.

6   strips bacon, diced
¼   cup diced green pepper
1   medium onion, coarsely chopped
1   12-ounce can tomato soup
2   cups cooked rice
Tabasco sauce to taste, optional

Sauté bacon until crisp; remove and drain on paper towels. Meanwhile, add the diced pepper and onion to the bacon fat and cook over moderate heat until tender. Add soup, bacon bits, and rice to pan and mix well. Heat through. **Serves 6.**

CHEESE

BAKED BRIE

1   1-kilogram (35.2-ounce) wheel Brie cheese
1   tablespoon butter
½   cup slivered almonds

Preheat oven to 350° F. With a sharp knife, cut the top portion of rind away from the cheese, leaving the rest of the shell intact. Dot with butter and top with slivered almonds. Place Brie on baking sheet and bake 20 minutes, or until cheese is melted. Transfer to serving dish. Serve with crackers as an appetizer, or spoon over steamed vegetables as a first course.

FRIED CHEESE

1   pound Jarlsberg or Baby Swiss cheese,
    sliced ³/₄-inch thick
Fresh French or Italian bread, broken into
    chunks

Heat a nonstick skillet very hot. Add cheese slices and
fry over medium high heat, turning once, until cheese
is crusty on the outside and melted on the inside. Serve
immediately with buttered bread. **Serves 4.**

PIROGI

4   large potatoes, cooked and mashed
³/₄ cup grated American cheese
2   cups flour
1   egg
1   teaspoon salt
²/₃ cup water

Combine potatoes and cheese. Mound flour on work
surface. Make a well in the center; break the egg into
the well and add salt and a few tablespoons of water.
Beat egg with a fork. Gradually mix flour into egg with
fingertips, adding more water until mixture forms a

crumbly paste. Form dough into a ball and gently knead until smooth and elastic. Wrap dough in plastic wrap and allow to rest at room temperature 1 hour. Roll the dough out to $1/8$-inch thickness. Cut into 3-inch rounds. Working with one round at a time, place about 1 teaspoon potato filling in center of dough. Moisten the edges with water; fold dough over and pinch edges together. Boil pirogi in 4 quarts boiling water about 4 minutes. Serve well buttered. **Serves 4 to 6 as a side dish.**

RACLETTE

A giant hero sandwich!

> 1 **large loaf French or Italian bread, buttered and split lengthwise**
> $3/4$ **pound raclette cheese, sliced**
> 1 **large ripe tomato, sliced**
> $1/4$ **cup chopped scallions**

Preheat oven to 375° F. Place bread on a baking sheet. Layer cheese slices and tomato over bread. Sprinkle scallions on top and bake 20 minutes. An excellent dish to serve at a brunch or luncheon. **Serves 4 to 6.**

BASIC CHEESE SOUFFLÉ

With a loaf of good bread, and a salad or asparagus vinaigrette, this makes a great luncheon or light summer supper.

      3   **tablespoons butter**
      ¼   **cup flour**
      1   **cup milk**
      1   **cup grated cheese—American,
          cheddar, Swiss, or Stilton**
      6   **eggs, separated**

Preheat oven to 400° F. Butter the inside of a 1½-quart soufflé dish. In a medium saucepan, melt the butter; add the flour and cook over moderate heat about 2 minutes, stirring constantly. Do not let the mixture brown. Add the milk gradually while whisking to blend ingredients. Cook until mixture is very thick, about 10 minutes. Add the cheese and whisk to blend thoroughly. Remove from heat. Beat the egg yolks until thick and lemon colored. Add cheese sauce, beating continuously until well blended. Beat egg whites until very stiff; fold whites quickly but gently into cheese mixture. Pour into prepared soufflé dish. Run the tip of a teaspoon around the batter about 1½ inches from edge. (This forms the "top hat" effect when soufflé puffs.) Immediately place soufflé dish in middle of oven and turn heat down to 350° F. (Do not open door for at least 30 minutes.) Bake 40 to 45 minutes, or until top is nicely browned. Serve immediately. **Serves 4.**

Variations:
Add ½ cup finely chopped ham to cheese sauce before blending with egg yolks.

Add 1 pound fresh lump crabmeat to sauce containing Swiss cheese. Proceed as above.

On
the
Side

The right sauce, condiment, or side dish can turn a plain meal into an event. We have included serving suggestions for the recipes in this chapter, but feel free to experiment. Try serving a main dish of plain chicken or fish with an assortment of sauces—for dessert, plain pound cake or ice cream can be transformed in the same way. A handful of great sauce and dressing recipes can be used to make your cooking (and your meals) exciting and creative.

SAUCES AND DRESSINGS

ANCHOVY SAUCE

Delicious on any salad greens; but when you're feeling extravagant, prepare individual servings of red-leaf lettuce and sliced endive. Top with slivers of red pepper and pour anchovy sauce over all.

1   egg yolk
¼   cup red wine vinegar
1   large garlic clove
12 anchovy fillets
1   cup olive oil

Place egg yolk, vinegar, garlic, and anchovy fillets in work bowl of food processor or blender and process until smooth. With machine running, add oil in a thin stream and continue to process until thick. **Makes about 1¼ cups.**

AVOCADO-DILL SAUCE

1   large ripe avocado, peeled and pitted
1/4 cup sour cream
3   tablespoons fresh chopped dill
2   tablespoons lime juice
Tabasco sauce to taste

Combine all ingredients in work bowl of food processor
or blender and process until creamy. Great over hard-
boiled eggs or poached fish. **Makes about 1/2 cup.**

BÉCHAMEL SAUCE

Béchamel sauce is very versatile and lends itself to additional flavorings. Try adding 1/4 cup grated Parmesan
cheese, a pinch of nutmeg, or a few tablespoons cognac.

2   tablespoons sweet butter
2   tablespoons sifted all-purpose flour
2   cups hot milk
1   cup white wine or chicken stock,
     optional

Melt butter in a heavy pan over low heat; add flour and
cook slowly, stirring, until butter and flour are well combined, about 2 minutes. Do not allow mixture to brown.

Remove from heat, add milk all at once, and whisk vigorously to blend ingredients. Return pan to heat and cook gently 10 minutes, or until thick, stirring occasionally. If using white wine or stock, add and cook 5 minutes longer. Season with salt and pepper and a pinch of nutmeg, if desired. **Makes about 2 cups.**

QUICK BROWN SAUCE

2   teaspoons arrowroot
3   tablespoons water
2   cups hot canned beef broth

In a small bowl, combine arrowroot and water to form a paste. Stir arrowroot mixture into hot broth and simmer until sauce is thick. **Makes 2 cups.**

CHINESE DIPPING SAUCE

Try this recipe with prepackaged egg rolls, spareribs, or broiled chicken wings.

$1/2$ cup sugar
2   tablespoons cornstarch
1   teaspoon salt
2   cups hot water
3   tablespoons light soy sauce
Pinch cayenne powder

Combine sugar, cornstarch, and salt in small saucepan with ¼ cup hot water. Stir to make a smooth paste. Gradually add 1¾ cups hot water, stirring constantly. Add soy sauce and cayenne. Place over medium high heat, stirring constantly until sauce boils and thickens slightly. Remove from heat and cool to room temperature. **Makes about 2 cups.**

CRÈME FRAÎCHE

1   **cup heavy cream**
2   **tablespoons buttermilk**
Sugar or freshly grated nutmeg, optional

Pour cream and buttermilk into a glass jar and stir until well blended. Cover and let stand at room temperature in a draft-free area, stirring several times, until mixture has thickened, about 24 hours. Chill thoroughly before using. Serve with additional sugar and freshly grated nutmeg over berries, pancakes, or your favorite fruit pie. **Makes 1 cup.**

SAUCE FRAMBOISE

2   **10-ounce packages frozen raspberries**
    in syrup, partially thawed
½   **cup sugar**

Press raspberries through a fine sieve, extracting as much juice as possible. Discard seeds. Combine raspberry juice with sugar and stir until sugar dissolves. Chill until ready to use. Serve over custards, ice cream, or pound or angel cake. **Makes about 2 cups.**

FRENCH DRESSING

2   tablespoons fresh lemon juice
Salt and pepper to taste
$\frac{1}{2}$ cup olive oil
2   teaspoons Dijon mustard, or to taste

In a small bowl whisk together lemon juice, salt, and pepper. Add oil in slow stream, whisking constantly until oil has emulsified. Stir in mustard. **Makes about $\frac{1}{2}$ cup.**

LEMON DRESSING

3   tablespoons lemon juice
$\frac{1}{4}$ cup peanut, olive, or saffron oil
1   tablespoon minced parsley
1   tablespoon Parmesan cheese

Combine all ingredients in jar; cover and shake until well blended. **Makes about ½ cup.**

MAYONNAISE

1   **egg yolk**
1   **tablespoon vinegar**
1   **tablespoon Dijon mustard**
Salt and freshly ground pepper to taste
1   **cup vegetable or corn oil**

Put egg yolk in a medium mixing bowl, or work bowl of food processor fitted with steel blade, with vinegar, mustard, and salt. Beat with a wire whisk or process until yolk is thick and lemon colored. Add oil in a thin stream, beating continuously until mixture is thick. **Makes 1 cup.**

ANCHOVY MAYONNAISE
Add 1 tablespoon chopped anchovy fillets, and 1 sieved hard-cooked egg to prepared mayonnaise. Serve as a sauce for poached fish.

COGNAC COCKTAIL SAUCE
Add 1 tablespoon cognac and 1 tablespoon tomato paste to prepared mayonnaise. Serve with cold shrimp or crabmeat.

CUCUMBER MAYONNAISE

Add 1 cup peeled, seeded, and finely chopped cucumber to prepared mayonnaise. Serve over cold poached fish.

REMOULADE SAUCE

Add 1 tablespoon anchovy fillets, 1 teaspoon capers, and 1 tablespoon finely chopped pickles to prepared mayonnaise. Use in chicken or seafood salads.

WATERCRESS MAYONNAISE

Add ½ cup finely chopped watercress to prepared mayonnaise.

MELBA SAUCE

1   **10-ounce package frozen peaches**
1   **10-ounce package frozen raspberries**
1   **tablespoon cornstarch**
1   **tablespoon water**
2   **tablespoons kirsch**

Puree fruit in work bowl of food processor or blender until smooth. Transfer to saucepan and bring to a boil. In a small bowl combine cornstarch and water to form a paste. Stir into puree and cook 1 minute, or until thick

and clear. Strain sauce; add kirsch. Chill at least 1 hour.
Makes about 2^1/$_2$ cups.

MUSTARD VINAIGRETTE

3   **tablespoons Dijon mustard**
2   **tablespoons hot water**
^{1}/$_2$ **cup oil**
Lemon juice
Salt and freshly ground pepper

Stir mustard and water together in a small bowl. Gradually add oil, whisking constantly. Add lemon juice and salt and pepper to taste. **Makes about ^{1}/$_2$ cup.**

SAUCE MORNAY

Try adding a teaspoon of dry mustard for a variation on this classic sauce.

3   **tablespoons butter**
^{1}/$_4$ **cup flour**
2   **cups hot milk**
^{1}/$_2$ **pound sharp cheddar cheese,**
     shredded

Melt butter in a small saucepan over low heat. Add flour and whisk together for 2 to 3 minutes. Add milk and bring to a boil, whisking constantly, until sauce is thickened, about 1 minute. Remove from heat; add cheese and whisk until cheese melts. **Makes 3 cups.**

PESTO

To our way of thinking, pesto is one of the best sauces around. It can be used for hot and cold pasta dishes, as well as for seafood and chicken. It freezes well, too.

1   large bunch fresh basil, washed, stems removed
4   cloves garlic
$^{1}/_{4}$ cup pignoli (pine nuts)
$^{3}/_{4}$ cup Parmesan cheese
1   cup olive oil, or $^{1}/_{2}$ cup butter and $^{1}/_{2}$ cup olive oil

In work bowl of food processor or blender, chop basil leaves very fine; add garlic and process a few more seconds until well blended. Add nuts and cheese and process 1 minute. Add oil in a thin stream, continuing to process until all ingredients are thoroughly combined. Place pesto in a covered container; pour $^{1}/_{4}$ inch olive oil over pesto. Keeps for weeks in refrigerator. **Makes about 1$^{1}/_{4}$ cups.**

RUM SAUCE

For pound cake, ice cream, or steamed puddings.

- ¼ **cup butter**
- 1 **cup brown sugar, firmly packed**
- 2 **tablespoons unsifted all-purpose flour**
- 1 **cup water**
- ¼ **cup dark rum**

Melt butter with sugar over low heat. Add flour, stirring constantly. Add water gradually and continue to stir until mixture thickens. Remove from heat and add rum. Pour into a tightly covered jar and refrigerate up to 3 weeks. **Makes about 1 cup.**

SOY DRESSING I

- ½ **cup soy sauce**
- ¼ **cup sesame oil**
- 2 **teaspoons sugar**
- 2 **tablespoons vinegar**
- 2 **scallions, chopped**

Combine all ingredients and mix well. Serve over salad.
Makes about ¾ cup.

SOY DRESSING II

3   tablespoons wine vinegar or fresh
     lemon juice
3   tablespoons soy sauce
2   tablespoons vegetable oil
1/4 teaspoon curry powder
1/2 cup mayonnaise, optional

Combine all ingredients and mix well. Serve over cooked vegetables. **Makes about 1/3 cup.**

TOFU DRESSING

A great dip for fresh vegetables, or serve as thick dressing for salad.

1   8-ounce cake tofu (bean curd)
1   tablespoon sesame oil
2   teaspoons salt
2   tablespoons diced scallions
1   teaspoon grated ginger

Puree ingredients in blender or food processor. Serve immediately. **Makes about 1/2 cup.**

SAUCE VERTE

Sauce verte—green sauce. Try over salads or smoked fish.

- ¹/₂ **cup chopped watercress**
- 1 **tablespoon chopped fresh parsley**
- 1 **tablespoon chopped fresh tarragon leaves**
- 1 **tablespoon chopped fresh chives**
- 2 **cups mayonnaise**

Combine all ingredients and mix well. **Makes about 2 cups.**

SALADS AND SIDE DISHES

CROCK SALAD

A "bottomless" salad that will keep in the refrigerator up to a week.

- 2 **large tomatoes, sliced**
- 2 **large green peppers, sliced, seeds and ribs removed**
- 1¹/₂ **cups red wine vinegar**
- 1¹/₂ **cups salad oil**
- ²/₃ **cup sugar**

Combine all ingredients in crock; cover and chill at least 1 hour. Any combination of vegetables may be added to the crock; adjust seasoning accordingly.

CUCUMBERS WITH DILL

2	large cucumbers, peeled and thinly sliced
4	tablespoons white wine vinegar
1 to 2	tablespoons sugar, or to taste
2	teaspoons salt
1	tablespoon minced fresh dill

Combine all ingredients in a medium bowl; cover and chill at least 1 hour.

ORANGE-ONION SALAD

2	oranges
1	tablespoon mayonnaise
1/2	medium head lettuce, shredded
2	tablespoons finely minced onion
2	teaspoons sugar

Halve the oranges and squeeze the juice from one of the halves. Combine juice with mayonnaise and sugar. Peel and divide remaining orange halves into sections; combine with lettuce and onion. Top with dressing and toss. **Serves 4.**

PEANUT SLAW

Don't be put off by the rather strange combination of ingredients—it's great!

- 5   cups finely shredded cabbage
- 1   large banana, cut into ¼-inch rounds
- ⅓   cup chopped salted peanuts
- ½   cup mayonnaise
- ¼   cup orange juice

Combine all ingredients; cover and chill at least 1 hour. **Serves 6 to 8.**

SPICED PECANS

- ¾   cup sweet butter
- ½   teaspoon Tabasco sauce
- 1   teaspoon Worcestershire sauce
- 1   large clove garlic, finely minced
- 1   pound pecans, shelled

Preheat oven to 325° F. In a small saucepan, melt butter over low heat. Add Tabasco, Worcestershire, and garlic, and cook 2 minutes. Do not let garlic brown. Place pecans in one layer on jelly roll pan or baking sheet and pour butter mixture over. Bake 20 to 30 minutes, shaking pan occasionally. Serve hot or cold.

POTATO SALAD

It is true that this recipe has 6 ingredients, although the addition of the celery is optional. However, it's just too good a recipe to pass by. Try it and you'll never need another recipe for potato salad!

> 3 **pounds boiling potatoes, quartered**
> 1/2 **pound bacon, cooked, drained, and crumbled**
> 1 **medium yellow onion, diced**
> 3 **hard-cooked eggs, diced**
> 2 **medium stalks celery, diced, optional**
> 3/4 to 1 **cup mayonnaise, preferably home-made**

Drop the potatoes into 4 cups boiling water; cover and cook them about 25 minutes, or until fork tender. Drain and peel potatoes while they are hot. Slice potatoes about 1/8-inch thick and combine with bacon, onion, eggs, celery, and mayonnaise. Toss well. Season with salt and pepper if desired. **Serves 4 to 6.**

BROILED POTATO SKINS

Tired of french fries? Here's the answer.

- ¹/₄ **cup butter**
- **Skins of 8 large boiling potatoes, washed**
- 2 **scallions, chopped**
- 6 **strips bacon, cooked, drained, and crumbled**
- 1 **cup shredded cheddar cheese**

Preheat oven to broil. Heat butter in a medium skillet; add potato skins and scallions and cook over moderate heat 8 to 10 minutes, or until tender. Transfer to an ovenproof serving dish and top with crumbled bacon and cheese. Place under broiler until cheese is bubbly. **Serves 4.**

RADISH SALAD

- 1 **medium bunch radishes, washed, trimmed, and sliced**
- ¹/₃ **cup vinegar**
- 2 **teaspoons salt**
- 1 **teaspoon sugar**
- **Freshly ground pepper to taste**

Combine radishes, vinegar, salt, and sugar in a medium bowl. Allow to marinate 2 hours. Drain on absorbent paper, squeezing to remove excess vinegar. Add pepper to taste, and serve. **Makes about 4 servings.**

FRIED SWEET POTATOES

Try these with ham and eggs.

> 2 **large sweet potatoes, unpeeled, well scrubbed**
> **Oil for deep frying**
> **Salt and pepper to taste**

Slice the potatoes into ¼-inch strips. Dry thoroughly with paper toweling, squeezing to remove excess moisture. Fry in hot oil until tender but crisp. Drain; season with salt and pepper and serve. **Serves 4.**

PICKLES AND RELISHES

Don't let the idea of making your own pickles and preserves scare you. It's really one of the more satisfying cooking methods, and the results are worth the effort.

Homemade pickles and preserves are easy to make, great to have on hand, and make unique and much appreciated gifts.

PICKLED CHERRIES

5   **pounds fresh cherries, stems removed**
1   **pound sugar**
2   **quarts red wine vinegar**
4   **cinnamon sticks**

Pack cherries into 4 sterilized jars or 1 large container. In a 3-quart saucepan combine sugar, vinegar, and cinnamon over high heat, and bring to a boil, stirring frequently. Boil 5 minutes. Place 1 cinnamon stick in each jar and pour in syrup to within 1 inch of the top. Seal jars if desired.

NOTE: Cherries will keep in a covered plastic container in the refrigerator for 1 year.

Variations:
Pickled peaches or pears can be made in much the same way. Wash fruit thoroughly, remove stems. Prick whole pears all over with the tines of a fork before packing into jars. Pour boiling syrup over top and seal if desired. For pickled peaches, scrub fuzz off fruit and pit. Pack sliced peaches into jars before adding syrup.

PLAIN PICKLES

35   small cucumbers, 3 to 4 inches long
3   tablespoons mixed pickling spice
³/₄   cup sugar
¹/₂   cup salt
4   cups vinegar

Wash and dry cucumbers, and cut in half lengthwise. Set aside. Bring 4 cups water to a boil in a large saucepan. Tie spices in a cheesecloth bag. Add sugar, salt, vinegar, and spice bag to boiling water. Return water to boil slowly; reduce heat and simmer 15 minutes. Meanwhile pack cucumbers into hot, clean pint or half-pint jars. Add hot pickling liquid to within ¹/₂- inch of top, making sure that cucumbers are covered completely. Seal jars immediately and place in a large pan of boiling water. (There should be at least 2 inches of boiling water above the jars.) Boil for 15 minutes. Seal jars and store 3 weeks before using. **Makes about 10 pints.**

DILL PICKLES

To make dill pickles, simply add 1 head fresh dill to each jar with pickles. Pour brine over and process as usual.

SWEET PICKLES

Add ½ cup brown sugar and 1½ teaspoons turmeric to above recipe. Pack pickles with slices of white onion.

CRANBERRY-ORANGE-NUT RELISH

1   **pound fresh cranberries, rinsed and drained**
2   **navel oranges, quartered**
6   **tablespoons sugar**
⅓   **cup curaçao**
1   **cup chopped walnuts**

Place cranberries and orange quarters in work bowl of food processor or blender and grate fine. (If using a blender, you will need to do this in several batches.) Add sugar and curaçao, adding more sugar to taste if desired. Add walnuts just before serving. This will keep up to 1 week in the refrigerator. **Makes about 2 pints.**

PICKLED PEPPER RELISH

A great all-purpose relish for hot dogs, hamburgers, or cold meats. For mincing peppers and onions, we recommend a food processor. Otherwise, it can be a time-consuming and rather teary-eyed task.

> 4 **cups minced green peppers, or 2 cups minced green and 2 cups minced red peppers**
> 4 **cups chopped white onions**
> 1 **cup sugar**
> 1 **quart vinegar**
> 4 **teaspoons salt**

Put peppers and onions in a large saucepan. Add sugar, vinegar, and salt and bring to a boil over medium high heat, stirring until sugar dissolves. Continue cooking until liquid is reduced and mixture is slightly thickened. Pack into hot, clean jars and seal, if desired. Otherwise, this relish will keep, tightly covered, in the refrigerator for up to 6 months. **Makes about 4 pints.**

RED PEPPER JELLY

A great accompaniment to meats or with cheese and crackers as an hors d'oeuvre.

10   red peppers, washed, seeds and stems
     removed, minced
Salt
3   cups sugar
3/4 cup white vinegar

Place minced peppers in a bowl and sprinkle with salt.
Set aside for 6 hours. Rinse peppers well and drain.
Place peppers, sugar, and vinegar together in a large
saucepan and bring to a boil, stirring occasionally. Cook
uncovered for 30 to 40 minutes, or until mixture begins
to thicken. Skim off foam, pour into sterilized jars, and
seal. **Makes about 4 pints.**

JAMS AND PRESERVES

Like pickles, jams are fun to prepare and make great
gifts. Most of the recipes below rely on the addition of
lemon juice to provide the fruit pectin necessary to thicken
the jam. If you prefer, omit half the lemon juice and all
the rind called for in the recipes below, and substitute
1 package liquid or dry fruit pectin, proceeding according to package directions.

Cook jam quickly and not too long. To determine
the setting point, mix jam with a wooden spoon and lift
spoon over pot. If the drip coming off the spoon hangs
in sheets for a few seconds before falling into the pot,
the setting point has been reached. Making perfect jam
does take a little practice, so if you don't get it right the
first time, don't be afraid to pour too-thin jam back into
the pot and cook it a little longer. No harm done.

BANANA JAM

Try it, and you'll forsake plain old grape jam forever!

   6   medium bananas, peeled and sliced
1¼ cups water
   7   cups sugar
Juice and rind of 4 lemons

Place bananas in a large saucepan with water, sugar, and lemon juice. Cut rind into thin strips and tie loosely in a muslin or cheesecloth bag; add to pan. Bring mixture to a boil over medium high heat, stirring only until sugar dissolves. Reduce heat slightly and cook 2 minutes. Remove from heat, cover, and allow to stand overnight. The next day uncover and bring to a boil over medium high heat. Boil rapidly until setting point (see page 165) is reached, about 40 minutes. Pour into clean jars and seal. **Makes about 4 pints.**

SHERRIED FIG PRESERVES

Not only a great jam for toast and rolls, but a surprisingly good accompaniment to meats and poultry.

   2   pounds fresh figs, stems removed,
      washed, and sliced
 ¾ cup water
Juice and rind of 2 lemons
   3   cups sugar
 ¼ cup cream sherry

Put sliced figs, water, and lemon juice together in a large saucepan. Slice lemon rind and pith; tie loosely in a muslin or cheesecloth bag and add to pan. Bring to a boil over medium high heat; reduce heat, and simmer until figs are tender. Remove muslin bag and add sugar, stirring constantly until dissolved. Continue cooking until setting point (see page 165) is reached, about 20 minutes. Remove from heat and allow to stand 5 minutes; skim if necessary. Pack into clean, hot jars and add approximately 2 tablespoons sherry to each jar. Seal jar. **Makes about 3 pints.**

LEMON MARMALADE

The secret to perfect marmalade is to cut away the thick, pithy portion of the rind, leaving only very thin, almost transparent strips. Try a coarse grater or thin slicing blade on a food processor for best results. This extraordinary marmalade also doubles as a glaze for chicken or duck.

    3   **pounds lemons**
    6   **pints water**
   12   **cups sugar**

Halve lemons and squeeze out all the juice. Tie seeds and pithy portion of rind together in a muslin or cheesecloth bag. Cut remaining rind into thin strips. Combine water and rind in a large saucepan over low heat. Add muslin bag containing seeds and pith and continue cooking over medium heat until strips of rind are very tender, about 40 minutes. Add sugar and return to a boil over high heat, stirring only until sugar dissolves. Boil rapidly until marmalade reaches setting point (see page 165), about 20 minutes. Allow marmalade to cool 10 minutes before packing into jars. **Makes about 8 pints.**

GINGER LEMON MARMALADE

Add ½ cup chopped crystallized ginger to the above recipe, at the same time as sugar.

MIXED FRUIT MARMALADE

Any combination of lemons, grapefruit, oranges, or limes can be combined for great-tasting results. The total weight of the fruit should be about 3 pounds. Proceed as for lemon marmalade.

STRAWBERRY JAM

A perennial favorite. Strawberries are very low in natural pectin, so prepackaged pectin must be added.

   3½   **pounds strawberries, washed and hulled**

   6   **cups sugar**

   1   **package dry fruit pectin**

Put a layer of strawberries in a large saucepan; sprinkle with sugar. Repeat procedure with remaining strawberries and sugar. Allow to stand 2 hours. Place pan over low heat, stirring constantly until sugar is dissolved and berries begin to give off their juice. Increase heat to medium high. Bring mixture to a boil and cook 5 minutes. Add fruit pectin and return to a rolling boil. Boil hard 2 minutes. Remove from heat and allow to stand 5 minutes. Skim if necessary. Pack into hot, clean jars and seal. **Makes about 4 pints.**

Breads and Baking

What is more satisfying than turning out a crusty loaf of homemade bread, a batch of light-as-a-feather biscuits, or a tempting homemade dessert? Home baking needn't be an overwhelming task. There are just a few simple rules to remember in order to insure perfect results every time.

Know your oven. Oven temperatures differ according to age, type of oven, and use. If you are unfamiliar with your oven's heating habits, invest in an oven thermometer. To insure even baking, place pans in the center rack of the oven.

Know your ingredients. All our recipes call for all-purpose flour. If you choose to substitute different flours, do so with caution, as different flours will impart different textures to your baked goods. Unless otherwise specified, our recipes call for large eggs. If you use smaller eggs, add 1 or 2 tablespoons additional liquid to compensate.

Pan size is important, too. We have specified pan sizes wherever possible. Should you not have the correct size pan, you may use a slightly smaller or larger pan, but remember to adjust your cooking times accordingly. Also, if you use a glass pan, reduce the heat by 25° F.

We have also included recipes which call for homemade mixes. It is our experience that they are both easy to make and easy to use and have all the convenience of prepackaged mixes, without the addition of chemical preservatives. Properly stored in a tightly covered container, these mixes will keep up to 2 months.

BREADS AND BISCUITS

Homemade mixes are easy to make and use and can be put together at about half the cost of prepackaged baking mixes, without added chemicals and preservatives. Try some of the recipes below, and we can guarantee you'll be hooked!

BAKING MIX

For dumplings, biscuits, waffles, pancakes, and quick breads of all kinds. Use as you would any packaged mix.

- 6 **cups all-purpose flour**
- 3 **tablespoons baking powder**
- 1 **tablespoon salt**
- 1 **cup all-purpose shortening**

Sift flour, baking powder, and salt together 3 times. Cut in the shortening and blend until mixture is the consistency of fine crumbs. Store in covered, airtight container up to 4 months. **Makes 7 cups, or enough for about 4 dozen biscuits.**

SELF-RISING FLOUR

Another handy item to have around that you can make for less than the cost of the prepackaged version.

> 6 cups all-purpose flour
> 3 tablespoons baking powder
> 1 teaspoon salt

Sift all ingredients together and store as you would any flour. **Makes about 6 cups.**

BEST BISCUITS

> 2 cups all-purpose flour
> 3 teaspoons baking powder
> 1/3 cup butter, softened
> 2/3 cup plain yogurt

Preheat oven to 425° F. Sift flour and baking powder together 3 times into a bowl. Cut in softened butter with a pastry blender or 2 knives until the mixture is the consistency of coarse crumbs. Add the yogurt and stir with a fork to form a stiff dough. Drop by heaping tablespoons onto greased baking sheet—close together for soft-sided biscuits, or 1 inch apart for crusty ones—or gently form dough into a ball and put on a lightly floured surface. Knead lightly with fingertips 10 to 15 times. Roll dough 1/2-inch thick. Cut with a floured biscuit cutter or knife. Place on baking sheet as described above. Bake about 15 minutes, or until biscuits are golden brown. **Makes about 18 biscuits.**

EASY BISCUITS

2   **cups baking mix (see page 172)**
1   **cup sour cream**

Put baking mix in a bowl; add sour cream and stir with a fork to form a stiff dough. Form dough into a ball; place on a floured board and roll to 1/2-inch thickness. Cut with a floured 2 1/2-inch biscuit cutter or knife. Place on a greased baking sheet—close together for soft-sided biscuits, or 1 inch apart for crusty ones. Bake for 12 minutes, or until golden. Serve hot. **Makes 1 dozen.**

BEER BREAD

3 cups self-rising flour (see page 173)
2 tablespoons sugar
1 12-ounce can good quality beer (not light beer)
7 tablespoons butter, melted

Preheat oven to 350° F. Combine flour, sugar, and beer and mix thoroughly in a bowl. Pour into a well-buttered 9 by 5 loaf pan. Spoon half the melted butter over the top of loaf and bake 20 minutes. Brush loaf with remaining butter and bake an additional 25 minutes. **Makes 1 loaf.**

BASIC BROWN BREAD

2 cups whole wheat flour
1 cup cornmeal
1 teaspoon baking soda
2 cups buttermilk
$^{1}/_{2}$ cup dark molasses

Preheat oven to 375° F. Combine whole wheat flour and cornmeal in a medium bowl and set aside. Add soda to buttermilk and allow to stand 5 minutes. Alternately add buttermilk and molasses to flours, mixing well after each addition. Bake in a well-greased, 9 by 5 by 2 loaf pan about 40 minutes, or until wooden pick inserted into center of bread comes out clean. **Makes 1 loaf.**

OATMEAL BREAD

1   **cup water**
3   **tablespoons butter**
³/₄   **cup rolled oats**
¹/₄   **cup blackstrap molasses**
1   **package dry yeast**
4   **cups sifted all-purpose flour**

Preheat oven to 375° F. In a large saucepan, bring 1 cup water to a boil. Remove from heat, add butter, and stir until melted; add oats and stir. Allow mixture to soak about 20 minutes, or until lukewarm. Stir in molasses and yeast; blend until yeast is dissolved. Add flour, 1 cup at a time, until mixture forms a stiff dough. Knead dough for 15 minutes by hand or 5 minutes in the work bowl of a food processor. Allow dough to rest 5 minutes. Turn into a greased bowl, cover with plastic wrap, and allow to rise in a draft-free place until doubled in bulk. Punch down; turn out onto a floured surface. Roll dough into a rectangle about 17 by 9; roll up to form a loaf, tucking in ends. Place in a well-greased 9 by 5 by 2 loaf pan and allow to rise again until doubled in bulk. Bake

at 375° F for 45 minutes, or until loaf is risen and brown.
Makes 1 loaf.

RICH BREAD

The evaporated milk substituted here for the whole milk
and butter usually found in other bread recipes pro-
duces a hearty, satisfying loaf. Though many bread recipes call for only 2 risings, we recommend a third rising,
since it yields a much lighter result.

³/₄ **cup warm water (105° to 115° F)**
1 **package dry yeast**
¹/₂ **cup evaporated milk**
1 **tablespoon sugar**
³/₄ **teaspoon salt**
5 to 6 **cups all-purpose flour**

Dissolve yeast in ³/₄ cup warm water. Heat milk just to
boiling; add sugar and salt and stir until dissolved. Allow to cool slightly; add yeast mixture and stir to blend.
Add flour, 2 cups at a time, blending with a spoon until
dough is stiff yet still easy to handle. Turn onto a floured
surface; knead for 10 minutes. Allow dough to rest 5
minutes. Place in a well-greased bowl, turning dough
once to grease the top. Cover with plastic wrap and
allow to rise in a warm place until doubled in bulk.
Punch down, turn, and allow to rise again until doubled
in bulk. Turn out onto a floured surface and pat down.
Allow to rest for 5 to 10 minutes. Form dough into 2

small loaves and place in well-greased loaf pans. Cover and allow to rise until doubled in bulk. Preheat oven to 400° F and bake 25 to 30 minutes, or until bread is golden brown. **Makes 2 loaves.**

The above recipe is a surprisingly versatile one, and lends itself to any number of delicious recipes:

ONION CHEESE LOAF

Roll dough into rectangle about 17 by 9 by 2; sprinkle with 1/2 cup shredded cheese and 1/4 cup sautéed onions. Roll up like a jelly roll to form loaf, being careful to seal the ends. Allow to rise and bake as above.

PAN PIZZA

Allow dough to rise only once. Pat down and roll dough to fit a 13 by 9 by 2 baking pan. Allow to rise 20 minutes; top with your favorite pizza toppings and bake at 425° F 15 to 20 minutes, or until crust is browned.

CLOVERLEAF HERB ROLLS

Add 1 tablespoon fresh snipped chives, 1 teaspoon dried oregano, and 1/2 teaspoon dried thyme to the above dough. Allow to rise as usual, then pat down. Form dough into 62 small balls; place 3 balls in each muffin-pan well (grease bottoms only). Allow to rise again and bake 15 to 20 minutes. **Makes 2 dozen.**

CINNAMON ROLLS

Increase sugar to 2 tablespoons. Allow to rise as usual. Pat down and roll into 14 by 9 by 2 rectangle. Sprinkle with ¼ cup sugar and 1 tablespoon cinnamon. Roll dough up like a jelly roll. Slice dough ½ inch thick and place rolls in a well-greased round cake pan. Allow to rise and bake as above. Ice if desired. **Makes approximately 2 dozen.**

CARAMEL PECAN ROLLS

Roll dough into 14 by 9 by 2 rectangle. Sprinkle with 3 tablespoons sugar and 2 teaspoons cinnamon. Roll up like a jelly roll and cut into ½-inch slices. Sprinkle ¼ cup brown sugar and ½ cup chopped pecans in a well-buttered 10-inch round cake pan. Place rolls on top of pecan mixture and allow to rise as usual. When rolls are done, invert pan immediately onto a plate.

FRENCH DOUGHNUTS

½ **teaspoon salt**
2 **tablespoons butter**
1 **cup all-purpose flour**
3 **eggs**
Oil for deep frying
Confectioners' sugar, optional

Place salt, butter, and 1 cup water in a large saucepan over low heat until butter is melted. Remove from heat. Add flour gradually, stirring constantly until mixture is smooth. Add eggs, one at a time, beating well after each addition. Cover dough and chill. Place dough in a pastry tube, and pipe into circles about 3 inches in diameter on a floured surface. Allow to dry 30 minutes. Meanwhile, heat oil to 350° F. Fry doughnuts, a few at a time, until light and golden. Drain and sprinkle with confectioners' sugar, if desired. **Makes approximately 1 dozen.**

SUPER MUFFINS

A light, sweet muffin, great for breakfast or an afternoon snack.

1   **pint vanilla ice cream, softened**
2   **cups sifted self-rising flour (see page 173)**

Preheat oven to 350° F. Combine softened ice cream and flour in a medium bowl, blending only until flour is moistened. Batter will be lumpy. Fill well-greased muffin tins ¾ full. Bake until muffins test done, about 20 minutes. **Makes 1 dozen.**

BASIC PANCAKES

2½   **cups baking mix (see page 172)**
2   **tablespoons oil**
¾   **cup milk**
1   **egg**

In a medium bowl, blend together all ingredients until moistened. Batter should be lumpy. Fry on a hot, greased griddle until bubbles form on the surface; turn and brown other side. **Makes about 2 dozen cakes.**

COTTAGE CHEESE PANCAKES
Decrease milk to ½ cup; add ½ cup large-curd cottage cheese to above batter.

BLUEBERRY PANCAKES
Add 1 cup fresh, washed blueberries to above recipe.

CHOCOLATE CHIP PANCAKES
Add 1 cup chocolate chips to above recipe, together with ½ cup chopped walnuts, if desired.

SCONES

- **2 cups all-purpose flour**
- **4 teaspoons baking powder**
- **4 tablespoons butter or shortening, softened**
- **2 eggs, beaten**
- **6 tablespoons milk**

Preheat oven to 425° F. Sift flour and baking powder together. In a separate bowl, blend shortening, eggs and milk. Add flour mixture gradually, adding more as needed to make a soft dough. Turn dough onto a floured surface; knead lightly until smooth. Divide dough in half and shape each into a round about 1/2-inch thick. Cut each round into 6 wedge-shaped pieces and bake on an ungreased baking sheet approximately 15 minutes. If desired, sprinkle with confectioners' sugar while still warm. **Makes 1 dozen.**

RAISIN NUT SCONES

Add 1/2 cup raisins and 1/2 cup chopped walnuts to above dough.

CHOCOLATE CHIP SCONES

Add 1 cup chocolate chips to above dough.

TORTILLAS

The results are fantastic, if a little difficult to achieve. Really a recipe for those days when you don't have anything else to do.

        1   **cup boiling water**
        1   **cup yellow cornmeal**
        2   **cups all-purpose flour**
        1/2 **teaspoon salt**

Pour boiling water over cornmeal and soak 20 minutes, or until mixture is cool enough to handle. Add flour and salt gradually, blending with the fingertips until mixture forms a stiff dough. Knead the dough 10 minutes. Cover with a damp cloth and allow to rest 5 minutes. Form dough into small balls. On a floured surface, roll the balls into 4-inch rounds, no more than $1/8$-inch thick. Cook on an ungreased griddle over medium heat for 2 minutes on each side. Use in any recipe calling for tortillas. **Makes about 12.**

CAKES AND COOKIES

CAKE MIX

6   **cups all-purpose flour**
4   **cups sugar**
3   **tablespoons baking powder**
2   **teaspoons salt**
1½ **cups all-purpose shortening**

Sift flour, sugar, baking powder, and salt together 3 times. Cut in shortening and blend until mixture is the consistency of coarse crumbs. Store covered in airtight container up to 4 months. **Makes about 12 cups, or enough for approximately 5 single-layer cakes.**

CARROT SNACK CAKE

4　carrots, trimmed and peeled
2¹/₂　cups cake mix (see page 183)
1　teaspoon cinnamon
1　egg
¹/₂　cup walnuts

Preheat oven to 350° F. Puree carrots in work bowl of food processor; add remaining ingredients and process until very smooth and light. Pour into prepared 8-inch square pan and bake for 30 minutes, or until cake tester or wooden pick inserted into center of cake comes out clean.

SINGLE-LAYER CHOCOLATE CAKE

2　cups cake mix (see page 183)
¹/₄　cup cocoa
1　egg
1　teaspoon vanilla extract
1　tablespoon confectioners' sugar

Preheat oven to 350° F. Combine mix, cocoa, and egg with ³/₄ cup water at low speed of electric mixer until well blended. Continue beating at highest speed an additional 4 minutes. Add vanilla and stir to blend. Pour into a greased and floured 8-inch round cake pan and bake until cake tests done, about 25 minutes. Sprinkle with confectioners' sugar, or, for a decorative touch, place a paper doily over top of cake, sift sugar over that, and remove carefully to stencil a lacy effect. **Makes 1 8-inch layer.**

CHOCOLATE CHIP CAKE

>   4   cups cake mix (see page 183)
>   2   eggs
>   1   cup milk
>   ²/₃ cup chocolate chips
>   2   teaspoons vanilla extract

Preheat oven to 350° F. Combine cake mix, eggs, and milk together at low speed of electric mixer until well blended, about 3 minutes. Continue beating at high speed for an additional 4 minutes. Add chocolate chips and vanilla and stir to blend. Pour into 2 prepared 8-inch layer cake pans and bake for 25 minutes, or until cake tests done. **Makes 2 8-inch layers.**

BANANA CHOCOLATE
CHIP CAKE

For a great variation, cut milk to ¾ cup and add 1 mashed ripe banana to the above mixture. Proceed as above.

EVERYDAY CAKE

2   **cups cake mix (see page 183)**
1   **egg**
½   **cup milk**
1   **teaspoon vanilla extract**

Preheat oven to 350° F. Combine cake mix, egg, and milk and beat at high speed of electric mixer until well blended, about 3 minutes. Add vanilla and blend. Pour into prepared 8-inch square or round baking pan and bake 25 minutes, or until cake tester inserted into center of cake comes out clean. **Serves 6 to 8.**

ANISE COOKIES

3 eggs
1 1/2 cups sugar
2 cups unsifted all-purpose flour
1 tablespoon anise seeds

Beat eggs and sugar together by hand or with a mixer until lemon colored. In a separate bowl, combine flour and anise seeds. Gradually beat into egg mixture and continue beating until well combined. With a pastry bag, pipe 1-inch circles onto greased cookie sheet, or put through a cookie press. Refrigerate uncovered 6 hours. Preheat oven to 300° F. Bake 12 to 15 minutes, or until lightly golden. May be stored in a tightly covered jar up to 1 week. **Makes 3 1/2 dozen.**

BUTTER COOKIES

1 pound sweet butter
1 cup sugar
1 teaspoon vanilla extract
1/2 teaspoon almond extract
4 cups unsifted all-purpose flour

Preheat oven to 325° F. Cream butter; add sugar gradually, beating until fluffy. Add extracts and blend. Add flour in fourths to make a smooth dough. Shape dough into 1-1/2 inch thick rolls, wrap in plastic wrap, and chill at least 3 hours. Slice rolls into cookies 1/2 -inch thick. Place on ungreased cookie sheet, and bake 12 to 15 minutes, or until lightly browned around the edges. **Makes about 5 dozen.**

Variations: If preferred, this dough can be put through a cookie press after chilling. Decorate or ice as desired.

THUMBPRINT COOKIES

Proceed as for butter cookies and chill. Roll dough into small balls. Make a depression in the center of each ball with your thumb, and fill depression with 1/2 teaspoon raspberry jam.

CLAIRE'S CRESCENT COOKIES

    2   cups all-purpose flour
    1/2   cup sugar
    1   cup butter, melted
    3/4   cup finely chopped walnuts
    1   teaspoon vanilla extract

Preheat oven to 350° F. Sift together flour and sugar. Add butter and knead until smooth. Add walnuts and vanilla and knead again until all ingredients are well blended. Chill about 1 hour. Roll dough into 1¼-inch balls, then into 3½-inch strips, then form into crescents. Bake on an ungreased cookie sheet until very lightly brown, about 12 minutes. While still warm, roll in powdered sugar, or a mixture of cinnamon and granulated sugar, if desired. **Makes about 3 dozen.**

EASY COOKIES

No baking, and delicious!

> 1 **6-ounce package peanut butter bits**
> ¾ **cups chunky peanut butter**
> 4 **cups cornflakes**

Combine peanut butter bits and peanut butter in a medium saucepan over low heat and cook until smooth. Remove from heat and fold in cornflakes. Spread in 8-inch square pan and chill. **Makes about 2 dozen.**

For a richer variation of the above recipe, melt 6 ounces of semisweet chocolate and 1 tablespoon butter together over low heat. When peanut butter mixture is firm, spread over top of cookies.

SALTED PEANUT COOKIES

14 ounces salted Spanish peanuts
3 eggs
1 cup brown sugar, firmly packed
3 tablespoons unsifted all-purpose flour
¼ teaspoon baking powder

Preheat oven to 350° F. Place peanuts in work bowl of food processor fitted with steel blade and process until finely chopped. Do not overprocess or you'll wind up with peanut butter. Add eggs and sugar and process a few seconds more. Add flour and baking powder and process until combined. Drop by tablespoonfuls onto ungreased baking sheet, and bake about 15 minutes, or until cookies are lightly browned. **Makes about 3 dozen.**

RYE COOKIES

½ cup butter, softened
⅓ cup sugar
1 egg
½ cup unsifted all-purpose flour
1 cup rye flour

Preheat oven to 400° F. Cream butter; add sugar gradually, beating until fluffy. Add egg to butter mixture and continue beating until light. Sift together flours. Add gradually to butter mixture, blending well to make a stiff dough. Shape dough into 2 1½-inch rolls. Wrap and chill overnight. Slice each roll crosswise into ½-inch rounds. Transfer to ungreased baking sheet. Bake 10 to 12 minutes, or until lightly browned. **Makes about 2 dozen.**

PIES AND PASTRY

First and foremost, we'd like to say that we're great believers in frozen pie crust. With the limited work space found in many kitchens, it's a great solution and saves time from what can be a chancy operation. Pie crust is like a number of other things—no one really seems to notice when it's perfect, they only notice when it's not! Nonetheless, for the fearless among you, the most important thing to remember about making pie crust is not to overhandle the dough. Flour and shortenings are to be blended only until they resemble coarse crumbs, and it is important to work quickly. Butter and shortenings should be chilled, and always use ice water for moisture. When liquid is added, blend only until crumbs are moistened before forming dough into a ball for rolling or chilling. Don't reroll trimming or scraps, it only toughens the pastry.

PIE PASTRY

3   cups all-purpose flour
1/2 teaspoon salt
9   tablespoons chilled butter, cut into 1/2-inch bits
1/4 cup shortening
1   egg plus 1 yolk, lightly beaten

Sift flour and salt together into a large bowl. With 2 knives or a pastry blender, cut in butter and shortening until mixture resembles coarse crumbs. Add egg and enough ice water to moisten ingredients (3 to 4 tablespoons). Mix lightly with a fork. Add only enough water to hold pastry together. Shape dough into a ball and flatten on a lightly floured surface. Wrap in waxed paper and chill at least one hour. When dough is ready to be rolled, lay it on a lightly floured surface. Divide dough in half. Place one half in refrigerator. (If you need only 1 shell for immediate use, wrap remaining half in plastic wrap and freeze up to 2 weeks.)

Roll dough from center to edge into a round about 1/8-inch thick and about 1 inch larger than overall size of the pan. Using a spatula, fold pastry in half, then gently lift and fit into pan. Unfold pastry carefully, so as not to stretch or tear it. Press dough lightly into bottom of pan; trim edge, if necessary, so pastry extends about 3/4 inch beyond edge of pan. Fold pastry under at edge and flute. Thoroughly prick bottom and sides of shell with a fork. (If filling is to be baked in shell, omit pricking.) To prevent sides of pastry from shrinking, line pastry with buttered wax paper: Cut paper 1 inch larger than size of pan and press it into pie pan; fill with dried beans or uncooked rice. Bake on middle shelf of a preheated 425° oven 10 to 15 minutes, or until crust is golden brown. Remove paper and beans. Cool on a rack. (For a partially cooked shell, bake 6 to 7 minutes, or until pastry has set.) **Makes 2 9-inch crusts, or 1 9-inch crust and lattice top.**

SWEET PASTRY

The butter and sugar used in this recipe combine to form a flaky, almost foolproof result. Though pastry can be made by hand, we recommend the use of a food processor to cut in butter.

$1^1/_2$ **cups all-purpose flour**
  2   **teaspoons sugar**
 10   **tablespoons chilled butter, cut into**
     $^1/_2$-inch bits

Sift flour and sugar together in a bowl. Cut in butter with a pastry blender, or in work bowl of food processor fitted with a steel knife, until mixture resembles coarse crumbs. Add ice water, 1 tablespoon at a time, until ingredients are moistened enough to press into a ball (3 to 4 tablespoons). Refrigerate pastry at least 1 hour. When dough is ready to be rolled, lay it on a lightly floured surface. Divide dough in half. Place one half in refrigerator. (If you need only 1 shell for immediate use, wrap remaining half in plastic wrap and freeze up to 2 weeks.)

Follow instructions for rolling and baking on pages 192–193. **Makes 2 9-inch crusts, or 1 9-inch crust and 1 lattice top.**

WHOLE-WHEAT PASTRY

Though this can be used for fruit pies and sweets, we think it's best when used for meat pastries or turnovers.

> $^3/_4$　**cup whole-wheat flour**
> $^2/_3$　**cup all-purpose flour**
> $^1/_2$　**teaspoon salt**
> 6　**teaspoons chilled butter, cut into $^1/_2$-inch bits**

Sift flours and salt into a large mixing bowl. Add butter and, working with pastry blender or fingertips, quickly work the mixture until it is the consistency of coarse crumbs. Add ice water, 1 tablespoon at a time, until dough is just moist enough to hold together. Knead dough for a few seconds until it forms a smooth, round ball. Cover with plastic or waxed paper and refrigerate 1 hour. When dough is ready to be rolled, lay it on a lightly floured surface.

Follow instructions for rolling and baking on pages 192–193. **Makes enough pastry for a 10-inch pie, or about 1 dozen, 3-inch turnovers.**

COCONUT CRUST

The easiest and one of the best crusts of all. Use for cream pies, ice cream pies, or chiffon pies.

> 1 **cup shredded sweetened coconut**
> ¼ **cup melted butter**

Preheat oven to 350° F. Combine coconut and butter until well blended. Press into a 9-inch pie plate and bake until golden, about 15 minutes. Cool before filling.

FRENCH APPLE TART

4   apples (Delicious, McIntosh, or
     Granny Smith are best)
1   recipe sweet pastry (see page 193) or 1
     10-inch frozen deep-dish pie crust, de-
     frosted
2   tablespoons butter, cut into $1/2$-inch bits
$1/4$ cup sugar
1   tablespoon confectioners' sugar,
     optional

Preheat oven to 375° F. Peel, core, and slice the apples
into $1/4$-inch wedges. Arrange pastry in a 10-inch pie pan.
Arrange apple slices in a circular pattern over bottom
of crust. Continue to layer slices in circles until all apples
are used. Dot with butter and sprinkle sugar over all.
Place on center rack of oven and bake 50 minutes, or
until crust is golden and apples are tender. Dust with
confectioners' sugar before serving, if desired. **Serves 8
to 10.**

FRESH FRUIT PIE

3   cups fresh fruit (such as apples, berries, peaches)

³/₄   to 1 cup sugar, depending on sweetness of fruit

3   tablespoons all-purpose flour

¹/₄   cup butter, cut into ¹/₂-inch bits

2   9-inch pie crusts, unbaked

Preheat oven to 400° F. Peel and slice fruit; combine with flour, sugar, and a pinch of salt. Spread fruit evenly into unbaked pastry and dot generously with butter. Fit second crust over pie and crimp edges to seal. Make 1 or 2 slashes in top crust to allow steam to escape. Bake on center rack of oven 50 to 60 minutes, or until crust is golden. **Serves 6 to 8.**

BUTTERSCOTCH PEACH PIE

2   cups peeled and sliced fresh peaches

¹/₂   cup dark brown sugar, firmly packed

¹/₄   cup butter

2   tablespoons flour

1   9-inch pie crust, baked

In a medium saucepan, heat peaches over low heat until they are slightly tender and begin to give off their juice. Add sugar and butter and stir until sugar dissolves. Blend flour with $1/4$ cup hot water and gradually add to peaches, stirring constantly over low heat until mixture starts to thicken. Cook 2 minutes. Remove from heat and pour into baked crust. Allow filling to set and cool before serving. **Serves 6 to 8.**

PEACH TART

8   tablespoons apricot preserves
1   9-inch pie crust, unbaked
3   tablespoons unsifted all-purpose flour
6   medium peaches, pitted and thinly sliced
2   tablespoons hot water

Preheat oven to 375° F. Thoroughly mix 3 tablespoons preserves with flour; spread evenly over bottom of pastry shell. Arrange peach slices in pie crust. Combine 2 tablespoons preserves with hot water; brush onto peaches. Bake tart 30 to 40 minutes. Cool. Melt remaining preserves in saucepan over low heat. Brush over baked tart. **Serves 6 to 8.**

Raspberry preserves may be substituted for the apricot preserves in the above recipe for a pretty, delicately tinted result.

PEANUT BUTTER PIE

3 **eggs**
$^1/_2$ **cup sugar**
$^1/_2$ **cup dark corn syrup**
$^3/_4$ **cup crunchy peanut butter**
1 **9-inch pie crust, unbaked**

Preheat oven to 325° F. Beat eggs until light and lemon colored; gradually add sugar and continue beating until slightly thickened. Add corn syrup in a thin stream, beating continuously. Add peanut butter and mix just until blended. Pour into crust and bake until filling is set, approximately 1 hour. **Serves 6 to 8.**

PECAN PIE

3 **eggs**
1 **cup dark corn syrup**
2 **tablespoons all-purpose flour**
1 **cup pecan halves**
1 **9-inch pie crust, unbaked**

Preheat oven to 325° F. Beat eggs until light; add corn syrup and flour and continue beating until well blended. Stir in pecan halves and pour into unbaked pastry. Bake until filling is set, 50 to 60 minutes. **Serves 6 to 8.**

PÂTÉ À CHOU

½   cup butter
1   teaspoon salt
1   cup all-purpose flour
4   eggs

Preheat oven to 425° F. In a medium saucepan, bring 1 cup water to a boil. Add butter and salt and stir until butter melts. Add flour all at once. Beat vigorously with a wooden spoon until mixture leaves sides of pan and forms a smooth ball. Remove from heat. Add eggs, one at a time, beating well after each addition. Continue beating until mixture is thick and smooth. Drop by tablespoonfuls onto an ungreased baking sheet. Bake for 15 minutes. Reduce heat to 350° and continue baking 20 minutes, or until puffs have doubled in size and are golden brown. **Makes 1 dozen puffs.**

CREAM PUFFS

Slice cooled puffs in half crosswise. Beat ½ cup heavy cream with 1 teaspoon corn syrup and 2 tablespoons confectioners' sugar. Fill each puff and replace top; dust with additional confectioners' sugar, if desired. Chill. **Makes 12.**

COFFEE PUFFS

Beat cream with 1 teaspoon powdered coffee.

CHOCOLATE PUFFS

Fill puffs with prepared instant chocolate pudding. Dust tops with confectioners' sugar or cocoa.

ECLAIRS

Using pastry bag, pipe dough onto baking sheet in wide strips, about 3 inches long. Bake as described on preceding page and fill with prepared instant vanilla pudding. Top with chocolate sauce or frosting.

Desserts

Anything worth doing, they tell us, is worth doing right. And when it comes to cooking for family or entertaining friends, it's worth it to include a great dessert. It doesn't have to be fattening, or even elaborate, but to finish your meals with a flourish, there's nothing like a touch of sweet to refresh the palate, lift the spirits, and add a touch of celebration to even the plainest everyday meal.

FRUIT DESSERTS

APPLE CRISP

½ cup butter, plus 2 tablespoons
½ cup sugar, plus 2 tablespoons
1 cup all-purpose flour, plus
   2 tablespoons
2 large apples, peeled, cored, and sliced
   ⅛-inch thick

1 teaspoon cinnamon

Preheat oven to 375° F. Combine ½ cup butter, ½ cup sugar, and 1 cup flour in a medium bowl until mixture is the consistency of coarse crumbs. Press half of mixture into an 8-inch square baking pan. In a separate bowl, combine apple slices and remaining 2 tablespoons each sugar, flour, and butter. Mix well. Layer evenly in pan and sprinkle with cinnamon. Top with remaining crumb mixture and bake 1 hour, or until apple slices are tender. **Serves 4 to 6.**

CHERRY CRISP

Omit apples and substitute 1 16-ounce can sour cherries, drained. Proceed as above.

PEACH CRISP

Omit apples and substitute 2 cups sliced fresh peaches, or 1 16-ounce can peaches, drained. Proceed as above.

BANANAS IN GINGER SAUCE

8   medium, very ripe bananas, peeled and
    cut into 1/4-inch rounds
1   tablespoon powdered ginger
1/2 cup sugar
1/2 cup water
1/4 cup lemon juice

Arrange half the banana slices decoratively on serving platter. Sprinkle 1/2 tablespoon ginger over bananas. Arrange remaining slices on top and sprinkle with remaining ginger. In a small saucepan, combine sugar and water and bring to a boil, stirring constantly until sugar is dissolved. Cook 8 to 10 minutes. Pour syrup over bananas and chill before serving. **Serves 8.**

BRANDIED PEARS

1   **cup dark brown sugar, firmly packed**
1/8   **teaspoon nutmeg**
4   **whole cloves**
4   **Bartlett pears, peeled**
1/4   **cup brandy**

Preheat oven to 350° F. In a flameproof dish combine sugar, 1 cup water, and nutmeg and bring to a boil. Boil 5 minutes. Insert cloves into pears. Add pears to dish and bake about 50 minutes, or until tender, basting occasionally. Remove cloves and transfer pears to serving dish. Add brandy to sauce, stir, and heat over low flame 1 minute. Pour sauce over pears. Serve immediately. **Serves 4.**

STRAWBERRIES ROMANOFF

1   **pint vanilla ice cream, softened**
1   **cup heavy cream, whipped**
1   **quart strawberries, mashed**
1/2   **cup confectioners' sugar**
1/3   **cup Cointreau or Grand Marnier**

Whip ice cream until creamy; fold in whipped cream. Combine strawberries, sugar, and orange liqueur in a small bowl; fold into ice cream. Serve in chilled stemmed glasses. **Serves 4 to 6.**

GINGERED SUMMER FRUIT

3 cups each cantaloupe and honeydew balls

3 kiwis, peeled and sliced

Lime juice to taste

4 slices fresh gingerroot, peeled and cut into size of a quarter

Combine all ingredients in a glass bowl and refrigerate at least 1 hour. Remove gingerroot before serving. **Serves 6.**

THE ONLY CHEESECAKE

Impressive on its own, this cheesecake can be made really dramatic by decorating with a variety of fresh fruit.

3 cups sour cream

1 pound fresh cream cheese (if unavailable, use softened packaged cream cheese)

1½ cups sugar

3 eggs

2 teaspoons vanilla extract

Preheat oven to 325° F. Put all ingredients in a large mixing bowl. Using high speed of electric mixer, combine until smooth and well blended. Pour into prepared graham or praline crust. Place on center rack of oven and bake until center of cake is set, about 1 hour. **Serves 6 to 8.**

PRALINE CRUST

2 **cups graham cracker crumbs**
$^1/_2$ **cup butter, melted**
3 **tablespoons brown sugar, firmly packed**
$^1/_2$ **cup ground walnuts**
$^1/_2$ **teaspoon cinnamon**

Mix all ingredients until well blended and press into bottom of 9-inch springform pan. Chill at least 15 minutes before using.

CAKES AND TORTES

NO-BAKE CHEESECAKE DELIGHT

This cake is cool and creamy—perfect for those hot days when you don't want to turn on the oven.

Crust:
- **24** **gingersnaps, finely crushed (about 1½ cups)**
- **6** **tablespoons melted butter or margarine**

Filling:
- **16** **ounces cream cheese, softened**
- **½** **cup honey**
- **16** **ounces plain yogurt**

Combine gingersnaps and butter in a bowl. Press into bottom of 10-inch springform pan. Place in freezer 15 minutes. In a medium bowl, combine cheese and honey until smooth and creamy. Gradually beat in yogurt just until smooth. Pour into crust. Cover and freeze until firm, about 4 hours. Let stand 15 minutes before serving. Serve immediately. This cake cannot stand at room temperature too long. Refreeze any uneaten portions. **Serves 10.**

CHOCOLATE TORTE

10 eggs, separated
1   cup sugar
6   ounces bittersweet chocolate, melted
    and cooled slightly
2   cups finely chopped walnuts (not
    ground)

Preheat oven to 350° F. Beat egg yolks; gradually add sugar and continue beating until thick and lemon colored. Stir in chocolate and nuts. Beat whites until stiff but not dry; fold into chocolate mixture. Pour into greased (bottom only) 10-inch springform pan and bake 1 hour. Cool on wire rack 10 minutes. Remove rim from pan and continue cooling torte to room temperature. If desired, garnish with a border of whipped cream. **Makes 8 to 10 servings.**

CHOCOLATE TRUFFLE CAKE

If desired, this can be served with a dollop of whipped cream, flavored with Kahlúa.

1   16-ounce package semisweet chocolate
     or chocolate chips
$1/2$ cup butter
$1^1/_2$ teaspoons sugar
$1^1/_2$ teaspoons all-purpose flour
4   eggs, separated

Preheat oven to 425° F. Heat chocolate and butter together over low heat until melted and smooth. Remove from heat and cool. Add sugar and flour; blend well. Beat in egg yolks, one at a time, beating well after each addition. Beat egg whites until stiff. Fold into chocolate mixture. Pour batter into a well-greased (bottom only) 8-inch springform pan. Bake 15 minutes. Center of cake should spring back slightly when pressed with fingertips. Do not overbake. Cool on wire rack 10 minutes. Remove rim from pan and continue cooling cake to room temperature. Chill thoroughly before serving. **Makes 8 to 10 servings.**

CHOCOLATISSIMO

10	ounces semisweet chocolate
1	teaspoon instant coffee powder
1¼	cups sweet butter, softened
1¼	cups sugar
10	eggs, separated

Preheat oven to 350° F. Melt chocolate with coffee in top of double boiler over hot, not boiling water. Stir until smooth; set aside to cool. Cream butter and sugar in a large bowl, using hand or electric mixer. Add cooled chocolate and blend well. Add egg yolks, one at a time, beating well after each addition for a total of 15 minutes. In another large bowl, beat egg whites until stiff but not dry. Fold into batter. Pour ¾ of batter into a greased (bottom only) 9-inch springform pan and bake 50 minutes. Set pan on wire rack to cool completely (cake will sink in the middle). Spread remaining uncooked batter over top of cake. Cover and chill overnight. Serve in thinly sliced portions. **Serves 12.**

FUDGE CAKE

This recipe forms its own filling, a fudgy tunnel in the center of the cake.

1½	**cups butter or margarine, at room temperature**
6	**eggs**
1½	**cups sugar**
2	**cups unsifted all-purpose flour**
1	**package dry fudge-frosting mix**

Preheat oven to 350° F. Beat butter until light and creamy. Beat in eggs one at a time, beating well after each addition. Beat in sugar, ¼ cup at a time. Stir in flour and frosting mix. Pour into a greased 10-inch tube pan and bake 60 minutes. Cool 10 minutes, then turn cake out onto rack to cool completely. **Serves 8 to 10.**

LEMON TORTE

1 cup sugar
6 eggs
¼ cup freshly squeezed lemon juice
2 tablespoons grated lemon peel
Sugar

Preheat oven to 325° F. Grease bottom of 15 by 10 by 1 jelly-roll pan. Line with wax paper cut to fit bottom of pan; grease paper. Set aside. Beat sugar and eggs together until very light. (Batter should be about the consistency of mayonnaise.) Fold in lemon peel and juice. Pour batter into prepared pan; bake 12 to 15 minutes, or just until top billows and turns a light brown. Remove from oven. Loosen edges of torte immediately and turn onto a towel. Peel off paper and sprinkle generously with sugar. To roll, begin at shorter side of torte. Using towel as a guide, tightly grasp towel and quickly pull it over beyond opposite edge. Torte will roll itself as you pull. Wrap roll in towel and cool on wire rack 4 to 6 hours. Remove towel and sprinkle with additional sugar, if desired. **Serves 6.**

MEXICAN WEDDING CAKES

Whether you call these cakes or cookies really depends on how big you make them—at any rate, they're delicious! Walnuts may be substituted for the pecans, but unfortunately they don't have quite the same mouth-watering tenderness.

¹/₂	cup sweet butter, softened
1	cup unsifted all-purpose flour
1¹/₄	cup confectioners' sugar
³/₄	cup ground pecans
¹/₂	teaspoon vanilla extract

Preheat oven to 350° F. Beat butter until light and creamy. Thoroughly mix flour with ³/₄ cup sugar; add to butter and blend until consistency of coarse crumbs. Add pecans and vanilla to form a smooth dough. Roll into 1-inch balls; place on ungreased cookie sheet and bake 10 to 12 minutes, or until cookies are very lightly browned. Roll in remaining powdered sugar while warm. Cool on wire rack. **Makes about 3 dozen cookies.**

MYSTERY CAKE

Though we tend to frown on packaged mixes, this recipe has never disappointed us!

1	18¹/₂-ounce package cake mix, choco-late-fudge flavor
1	3¹/₂-ounce package chocolate-fudge pudding mix
³/₄	cup mayonnaise (no substitutes)
4	eggs

Preheat oven to 350° F. Combine all ingredients and beat at high speed of electric mixer 4 to 5 minutes. Pour into a well-greased 7½ by 12 by 2 baking pan and bake until tester comes out clean. Sprinkle with powdered sugar, if desired. **Serves 8 to 10.**

MOLDED RASPBERRY CAKE

A bit elaborate, but well worth the effort.

> 8   **10-ounce packages frozen raspberries in syrup, thawed**
> 3   **3-ounce packages ladyfingers, split in half**
> **Cointreau**
> 2   **cups heavy cream**
> 1   **ounce candied violets, optional**

Let raspberries drain in a strainer 1 hour. Lightly brush ladyfingers with Cointreau. Line bottom and sides of a 12 by 4 by 2½ bread pan with ladyfingers. Spoon ⅓ of raspberries over ladyfingers. Top with another layer of ladyfingers. Repeat process twice to fill pan. Trim ladyfingers flush with edge of pan. Cover tightly with foil, so pan can be inverted. Refrigerate overnight, turning cake over several times. When ready to serve, remove foil and invert pan onto serving plate. Whip cream with ¼ cup Cointreau and spread heavily over sides and top. Garnish with candied violets, if desired. **Serves 6 to 8.**

OLD-FASHIONED SPONGE CAKE

4 eggs, separated, at room temperature
1 cup sugar
Juice and grated rind of 1 large lemon
1 cup sifted all-purpose flour
Pinch salt

Preheat oven to 325° F. In a medium bowl, beat yolks with hand beater or electric beater at high speed until thick and lemon colored. Gradually add sugar in a stream, beating constantly. Yolks should be thick and the consistency of mayonnaise. Beat in lemon juice and rind. In a separate bowl, beat egg whites until stiff but not dry. Stir ¼ of whites into yolks. Fold in remainder of egg whites. Sprinkle flour and salt on top of egg mixture and gently fold into egg mixture. Pour into an ungreased 9-inch tube pan and bake about 1 hour, or until cake tests done. Immediately invert cake onto rack and cool completely. **Serves 8 to 10.**

MERINGUES

Meringues are a very versatile dessert that can be filled with any number of wonderful combinations of ingredients. They are easy to make, low in calories, and lend themselves to very impressive desserts.

MERINGUE NESTS

3   egg whites
1/4   teaspoon salt
7   tablespoons sugar

Preheat oven to 425° F. Line a baking sheet with wax paper. Set aside. Beat egg whites and salt together until whites stand in stiff peaks. Continue beating, adding sugar 1 tablespoon at a time, until meringue is stiff and glossy. Using a large spoon, divide meringue into 4 equal portions on baking sheet, about 4 inches apart. Make a depression in the center of each meringue, building up sides. Each meringue nest should be 2 to 3 inches in diameter. Place baking sheet in oven and immediately reduce temperature to 250° F. Bake 40 minutes, or until meringues are golden. Turn oven off and allow meringues to dry undisturbed until oven is cool. **Makes 4.**

MERINGUES AU CHOCOLATE

4   meringue nests
1   pint vanilla ice cream
2   fresh peaches, pitted and sliced
Chocolate syrup

Spread 1 to 2 tablespoons chocolate syrup in depression of each meringue nest. Fill chocolate-lined nests with peach slices. Top with a scoop of vanilla ice cream and additional syrup. **Serves 4.**

SCHAUM TORTE

4   **meringue nests (see page 217)**
1   **pint fresh strawberries**
1/2   **pint heavy cream**
Sugar

Wash, hull, and slice the strawberries, reserving 4 perfect berries for garnish. Place berries in a bowl and sprinkle with 1/4 cup sugar; refrigerate. When ready to serve, whip the cream and sweeten with additional sugar, if desired. Divide berries equally into meringue nests, top with cream, and garnish. **Serves 4.**

MERINGUE COOKIES I

For a light and less elaborate dessert, meringues can be combined with any number of ingredients to make cookies. Prepare meringue batter as described on page 217. Fold in any combination of the following ingredients:

$^1/_2$ **cup chocolate chips**
$^1/_2$ **cup pecans or walnuts**
$^1/_2$ **candied fruit**
$^3/_4$ **cup coconut**

Place in heaping tablespoonfuls on a wax-paper-lined baking sheet. Place baking sheet in oven and immediately reduce temperature to 250° F. Bake 40 minutes, or until meringues are golden. Turn oven off and allow meringues to dry undisturbed until oven is cool. **Makes about 2 dozen.**

MERINGUE COOKIES II

2 **egg whites**
$^1/_2$ **cup sugar**
$^1/_2$ **cup chopped almonds**
$^1/_2$ **cup semisweet chocolate, cut into bits**

Preheat oven to 250° F. Beat whites until stiff; add sugar 1 tablespoon at a time and continue beating until whites are shiny. Fold in nuts and chocolate. Drop onto greased cookie sheet and bake 1 hour. **Makes about 2 dozen cookies.**

ICE CREAMS AND FROZEN DESSERTS

INSTANT ICE CREAM

1   cup heavy cream, well chilled
1/3   cup sugar
1   pound frozen unsweetened straw-
     berries

Place cream and sugar into work bowl of food processor fitted with steel knife and process until thickened. Add frozen fruit a few pieces at a time, and blend until smooth. Be careful not to overblend. Mixture should be the texture and thickness of a soft-serve ice cream. Serve immediately. **Serves 4.**

NOTE: With the help of a hand-held immersion blender, this ice cream recipe becomes quite thick and more the texture of conventional ice creams.

KAHLÚA CREAM

6   egg yolks, at room temperature
4   tablespoons sugar
4   tablespoons water
1/3   cup Kahlúa
3/4   cup heavy cream
1/3   cup chopped pecans, optional

In a medium bowl, beat egg yolks until lemon colored, about 15 minutes. In a small saucepan, combine sugar and water over low heat until sugar dissolves. Bring mixture to a boil and boil, without stirring, 4 minutes. Add syrup to egg yolks in a thin stream, beating continuously until mixture is cold. Stir in Kahlúa. Whip cream until soft peaks form. Gently fold into egg-yolk mixture; fold in pecans, if desired. Spoon into 4 sherbet glasses and freeze 3 to 4 hours or overnight. **Serves 4.**

FROZEN LEMON CREAM

An excellent low-calorie dessert.

> **2 cups nonfat milk**
> **¹/₂ cup sugar**
> **Juice and finely grated peel of 2 large lemons**
> **5 large lemons**

In a shallow pan, combine milk, sugar, lemon juice, and lemon peel, stirring until sugar dissolves. Place in freezer until cream is frozen. Cut remaining lemons in half lengthwise; remove pulp and refrigerate for another use. Place lemon shells in freezer. Transfer frozen cream to work bowl of food processor or blender and process until smooth. Return cream to freezer until partially frozen; fill lemon shells with partially frozen cream and refreeze until ready to serve. **Makes 10 lemon shells.**

LEMON-GINGER ICE CREAM PIE

A fantastically simple recipe with just the right combination of flavors—perfect for a cool summer dessert.

18   gingersnaps, crushed
¼   cup butter, melted
1   quart lemon ice cream or lemon sherbet, slightly softened.
Fresh peach slices or candied lemon peel for garnish

Preheat oven to 300° F. Combine gingersnap crumbs and melted butter. Press into a 9-inch pie plate and bake 10 minutes. Cool completely. Fill crust with softened ice cream or sherbet. Freeze 1 hour before serving. Garnish with fresh peach slices or lemon peel before serving. **Serves 6 to 8.**

PRALINE ICE CREAM

1⅓   cups sugar
3   tablespoons water
1   cup chopped almonds, toasted
6   cups heavy cream
¼   teaspoon salt

In a medium saucepan, boil ²/₃ cup sugar with water, stirring constantly until sugar caramelizes; remove from heat when color becomes light to medium brown. Stir in nuts immediately. Return to high heat and boil 2 minutes longer. Pour into a lightly buttered pan to cool completely. Break into pieces and place in work bowl of food processor or blender. Process until pulverized. Heat 2 cups cream until a shiny film has formed on top. Combine with praline, remaining sugar, and salt, and process until sugar dissolves. Cool to room temperature, then stir in remaining cream. Place in ice cream maker and churn according to manufacturer's directions. **Makes about 2 quarts.**

STRAWBERRY ICE CREAM

8 **cups fresh strawberries, washed, hulled, and quartered**
1¼ **cups sugar**
¼ **cup curaçao or Grand Marnier**
5 **egg yolks, lightly beaten**
1 **cup heavy cream**

Place strawberries in mixing bowl with sugar and orange liqueur. Stir gently, cover, and refrigerate 8 hours. Drain berries, reserving syrup. In a 2-quart saucepan combine syrup, egg yolks, and cream. Place over medium heat and cook, stirring constantly, until mixture is thick enough to coat a spoon. Do not allow to boil or sauce will curdle. Remove from heat and immediately place pan in cold water or over ice, stirring constantly until mixture has cooled. Place in ice cream maker and churn until partially frozen. Add strawberries and continue churning until mixture is firm. **Makes about 1¹/₂ quarts.**

VERY VANILLA ICE CREAM

A truly all-purpose ice cream that comes with a host of delectable variations.

> 2 **cups sugar**
> 2 **eggs**
> 1 **cup heavy cream**
> 1 **pint half and half**
> 1 **13¹/₂-ounce can evaporated milk**
> 1 **tablespoon vanilla extract**

Beat sugar and eggs together until very light; gradually add heavy cream and continue beating until mixture is thick. Add half and half and evaporated milk in a thin stream, beating continuously, and vanilla. (Mixture will be thin.) Pour into freezer compartment of ice cream maker and freeze according to manufacturer's directions. **Makes approximately 2 quarts.**

STRAWBERRY ICE CREAM

When mixture is partially frozen, add 1 10-ounce package partially thawed frozen strawberries. Replace cover on freezer and continue freezing until solid. To prepare with fresh strawberries: Wash and hull 1 pint berries; slice and cover with ¼ cup sugar. Add when mixture is partially frozen and continue freezing until solid.

CHOCOLATE CHIP ICE CREAM

Add 1 12-ounce package chocolate chips to partially frozen mixture. Continue freezing until solid.

PEACH ICE CREAM

Peel and dice 1 pound ripe peaches; sprinkle with ¼ cup sugar. Add to ice cream when partially frozen; continue freezing until solid.

COFFEE ICE CREAM

Dissolve 3 tablespoons instant coffee in ¼ cup hot water; add to basic ice cream mixture.

CHOCOLATE SHERBET

1¾   **cups unsweetened cocoa**
1   **cup sugar**
⅛   **teaspoon salt**
3½   **cups nonfat milk**
1   **vanilla bean**

Combine cocoa, sugar, and salt in a medium saucepan and mix well. Gradually stir in milk. Split vanilla bean; scrape out seed and add with bean to pan. Place pan over medium heat and bring to a boil, stirring constantly. Reduce heat and simmer, stirring constantly, 5 minutes. Let cool; remove vanilla bean. Pour into shallow pans and freeze. Spoon frozen sherbet into work bowl of food processor fitted with steel blade and process until smooth. May be served at this point or frozen further. **Makes 1 pint.**

Mousses, Puddings, and Soufflés

BASIC MOUSSE

6   egg yolks
½   cup plus 2 tablespoons sugar
1   quart heavy cream, chilled
½   ounce gelatin
    Flavoring (see list that follows recipe)

Put egg yolks and sugar in top of a double boiler and set over hot, not boiling, water. Remove from heat when yolks are warm, not hot. (They will begin to cook if hot.) Using a hand mixer or electric mixer, beat yolks at high speed until they are frothy and cold and have tripled in volume. Set aside. In a separate bowl, whip cream medium firm; set aside. Put ½ cup cold water in a medium saucepan; sprinkle in gelatin and place over low heat, stirring until gelatin has dissolved and liquid is clear. Remove pan from heat. Add flavoring to gelatin and mix well. Stir ⅓ whipped cream into egg yolks; stir a small amount of egg-cream mixture into gelatin. Add gelatin to remaining egg-cream mixture and fold in remaining cream. Transfer mousse to serving bowl or individual serving dishes. Refrigerate at least 3 hours. **Serves 6 to 8.**

Add any of the following:

6	ounces melted chocolate
	Juice and rind of 2 large lemons
	Rind of 2 oranges and juice of 1 orange
1½	pints strawberries, sliced
1½	pints raspberries, crushed

ONE-BOWL CHOCOLATE MOUSSE

6	ounces semisweet chocolate
3	tablespoons hot espresso coffee
2	eggs
¾	cup scalded milk
2	tablespoons orange liqueur or rum

Combine ingredients in work bowl of food processor or blender and process 2 minutes. Pour mixture into 6 stemmed glasses; chill at least 3 hours. **Serves 6.**

GRASSHOPPER MOUSSE

20	large marshmallows
¼	cup light cream
3	tablespoons crème de menthe
2	tablespoons crème de cacao
1	cup heavy cream, whipped

Combine marshmallows and light cream in a medium saucepan and stir over moderate heat until melted and smooth. Remove from heat and add liqueurs. Pour into a medium bowl, cover, and chill until soft-set. Fold into whipped cream, then spoon into long-stemmed sherbet glasses. Chill until set, garnishing with a sprig of fresh mint if desired. **Serves 6.**

RICE PUDDING

The secret of this recipe is to beat the eggs separately—then add the milk to the eggs.

2	quarts milk
1	cup sugar
1	cup uncooked rice
2	eggs
2	teaspoons vanilla extract
1¹/₂	teaspoons cinnamon, optional

In a large saucepan, heat milk just to boiling. Add sugar and rice and stir to blend. Reduce flame to low. In a separate bowl, beat eggs until light. Gradually pour about 1 cup of hot milk mixture and vanilla into eggs and blend thoroughly. Add entire egg mixture to saucepan. Cook for 1 hour over a low flame. (Mixture will not be thick.) Pour into a 2-quart casserole and allow to set at room temperature. Sprinkle with cinnamon, if desired. Serve warm or cold. **Serves 12.**

SYLLABUB

1   cup heavy cream, chilled
$^1/_3$ cup sugar
$^1/_3$ cup brandy or champagne
Juice and rind of 2 large lemons
2   egg whites

Combine cream and sugar in a medium bowl and beat until stiff. Stir in brandy, lemon juice, and rind. Beat egg whites in a separate bowl until soft peaks form; fold into cream mixture. Spoon into sherbet glasses and chill thoroughly. **Serves 4 to 6.**

CHOCOLATE CHEESE SOUFFLÉ

8   ounces cream cheese
$^1/_2$ cup light cream or milk
6   ounces semisweet chocolate
4   eggs, separated
1   tablespoon sugar

Preheat oven to 375° F. Butter a 1½-quart soufflé dish and dust it with sugar. Put cream cheese, light cream, and chocolate in a small saucepan and place over low heat, stirring continuously, until chocolate is melted and mixture is smooth. Remove from heat. In a separate bowl, beat egg yolks until thick. Gradually add to chocolate mixture, beating until well blended. Beat egg whites until foamy; add sugar and continue beating until stiff but not dry. Fold egg whites into chocolate-cheese mixture. Pour batter into soufflé dish; place on center rack in oven and bake 45 minutes. Serve immediately. **Serves 6.**

PEANUT BUTTER SOUFFLÉ

**3   tablespoons finely chopped unsalted
      peanuts**
¹⁄₂   cup creamy peanut butter
7   egg whites, at room temperature
7   tablespoons sugar
Sweetened whipped cream

Preheat oven to 400° F. Generously butter a 1-quart soufflé dish. Sprinkle bottom and sides with peanuts. Place peanut butter in a medium bowl. Beat egg whites in a large bowl until frothy; gradually add sugar and beat until soft peaks form. Stir about 1 cup whites into peanut butter; beat until smooth and evenly colored. Fold in remaining whites, gently and thoroughly. Turn into soufflé dish and place on center rack in oven. Immediately reduce temperature to 375° F. Bake 12 to 14 minutes, or until top is golden brown and cracked. Inside of soufflé should be soft. Serve immediately with sweetened whipped cream. **Serves 6 to 8.**

Cooking
for One
or Two

The task of cooking for one or two people doesn't have to result in boring food. In fact, one of life's greater pleasures can be the result of taking time out to prepare and enjoy a meal in the pleasure of your own company. Because singles and couples do have less time for such pleasures, however, we have attempted to include here recipes that provide great meals with a minimum of time and preparation. Don't be afraid to experiment, though. Most recipes can be cut in half with good results. Or, if you prefer, make double quantities ahead of time and store in your freezer. Whatever your method for cooking in small quantities, enjoy.

BACON-CHEESE CHOWDER

4	slices bacon
$^1/_2$	cup minced onion
3	cups milk
2	tablespoons all-purpose flour
$1^1/_4$	cups grated sharp cheddar cheese

Sauté bacon until crisp; remove from pan, drain on absorbent paper, and crumble. Add onion to bacon fat remaining in pan and sauté until translucent. Meanwhile, in a medium saucepan heat $2^1/_2$ cups milk over low heat. In a small bowl, gradually stir $^1/_2$ cup milk into flour to form a thin paste. Add bacon, onion, and flour paste to hot milk. Raise heat to medium and cook, stirring constantly, until chowder has thickened slightly. Add cheese and stir until melted. Heat through, but do not allow to boil. **Serves 2.**

CHICKEN GUMBO

1¹/₂ cups chicken stock, homemade or
      canned
1 6-ounce can chunk chicken
1 7-ounce package frozen okra, or 8
   ounces fresh okra, washed, trimmed,
   and cut into ¹/₄-inch rounds
1 16-ounce can tomatoes, undrained
1 tablespoon gumbo filé (available in
   specialty shops)

Combine all ingredients together in a large saucepan
and bring to a boil. Cover, reduce heat to low, and
simmer 45 minutes, stirring occasionally, or until sauce
is slightly thickened. **Serves 2.**

DINNER FOR ONE SOUP

For the next time you want to be good to yourself . . .

1 teaspoon caviar
1 teaspoon dry sherry
1 cup chicken broth, homemade or
   canned
1 tablespoon sour cream
Pinch paprika

Stir caviar, broth, and sherry together in serving cup; chill. When ready to drink, top with sour cream and paprika. **Serves 1.**

MUSHROOM SOUP

   3 **tablespoons butter**
  $^1/_3$ **cup mushrooms, sliced**
  $1^1/_3$ **cup chicken stock, homemade or canned**
   2 **egg yolks**
  $^1/_2$ **cup light cream or milk**

In a medium saucepan, melt butter; add mushrooms and sauté until liquid is absorbed and mushrooms are tender. Remove pan from heat. Pour chicken stock into work bowl of a food processor or blender; add mushrooms and process until mushrooms are chopped. Add egg yolks and process 30 seconds. Pour mixture into saucepan; add cream, and stir over heat until mixture thickens. **Serves 2.**

ONION SOUP AU GRATIN

> 1   **tablespoon butter**
> 1/2 **cup thinly sliced onion (1 small)**
> 2   **cups beef stock, homemade or canned**
> 2   **thick slices of French or Italian bread**
> 1/2 **cup grated Swiss cheese**

Preheat oven to broil. Over moderate heat, sauté onion in butter until lightly browned. Meanwhile, heat stock in a medium saucepan. Add onion to stock, cover, and simmer 20 minutes. Place a slice of bread in the bottom of each of 2 ovenproof soup bowls; top with grated cheese. Pour hot soup over. Place soup bowls on baking sheet and place under broiler for 3 minutes, or until cheese is browned. **Serves 2.**

PEACH SOUP

> 1/2 **pound fresh, ripe peaches, peeled and pitted**
> 2   **teaspoons lemon juice**
> 2   **tablespoons kirsch**
> 1/4 **cup heavy cream**

Combine peaches, lemon juice, and kirsch in work bowl of a food processor or blender and process until smooth. Add heavy cream and process just until well blended. **Serves 2.**

SALADS

CRABMEAT SALAD

1   6½-ounce can crabmeat
½   teaspoon lemon juice
2   tablespoons mayonnaise
¼   cup chopped celery

Thoroughly mix together all ingredients in a small bowl; toss well. Refrigerate at least 30 minutes before serving. **Serves 2.**

DAVID'S CHICKEN SALAD

1   chicken breast, about 4 ounces, cooked and cut into 1-inch cubes
2   teaspoons capers
½   teaspoon Dijon mustard
¼   cup mayonnaise
    Juice of ½ lemon

Thoroughly mix together all ingredients in a small bowl. Chill at least 30 minutes. **Serves 1.**

CUCUMBER SALAD

1/3   cup red wine vinegar
1   teaspoon salt
1   teaspoon sugar
2   Kirby cucumbers, cut into 1/2-inch rounds and quartered
3   tablespoons sesame seeds, toasted

In a small bowl, combine vinegar, salt, and sugar and mix until sugar dissolves. Add cucumbers and sesame seeds and toss well. Serve chilled. **Serves 2.**

PASTA WITH TUNA AND OLIVES

2   ounces ziti, cooked and chilled
1   3 1/2-ounce can tuna, packed in olive oil, undrained
1   scallion, sliced, top included
6   pitted black olives
Juice of 1 lemon

Thoroughly combine all ingredients in a small bowl. Garnish with chopped parsley, if desired. **Serves 1.**

SALMON SALAD

1   7½-ounce can pink salmon, drained
1   cup small shell macaroni, cooked
½   cup finely chopped green pepper
¼   cup sliced, pitted black olives
1   tablespoon bottled Russian salad
     dressing

Thoroughly combine all ingredients in a small bowl. Chill at least 30 minutes before serving. **Makes about 3 cups.**

COOL SHRIMP SALAD

½   medium ripe avocado
¼   pound shrimp, cooked
½   diced apple
¼   cup yogurt
4 or 5   fresh mint leaves, chopped

Thoroughly combine all ingredients in a small bowl. Chill at least 30 minutes. **Serves 1.**

BLUE CHEESE DRESSING

For a variation, try this.

- ¹/₂ **cup salad oil**
- 1 **teaspoon salt**
- ¹/₄ **cup vinegar**
- 3 **tablespoons blue cheese, crumbled**

Combine all ingredients in a jar; cover and shake well. Keep refrigerated, up to 1 month. Shake before serving. **Makes about ³/₄ cup.**

MUSTARD VINAIGRETTE

A great dressing for that staple of singles' cuisine . . . the salad.

- ¹/₄ **cup salad oil**
- ¹/₃ **cup lemon juice**
- 1 **teaspoon salt**
- ¹/₄ **teaspoon prepared mustard**

Combine all ingredients in a jar; cover and shake until thoroughly combined. Keep refrigerated, up to 1 month. Shake before serving. **Makes ³/₄ cup.**

HOT DISHES

TERIYAKI FOR TWO

1   pound sirloin, cut into 2-inch cubes
¼   cup brown sugar, firmly packed
½   cup soy sauce
1   large clove garlic, crushed
1   teaspoon grated gingerroot

Put all ingredients in a large bowl and toss to mix. Marinate at room temperature 2 to 3 hours, if time permits. About 20 minutes before serving, thread beef cubes on 4 short skewers. Baste with teriyaki sauce. Place under broiler or barbecue over coals, basting and turning often. To test doneness, cut a small slit in center of one cube, or press finger into cube. Medium-rare steak is pink in center and springs back when pressed. Serve skewered beef on a bed of hot rice and pour any remaining teriyaki sauce over all. **Serves 2.**

SAUTÉED VEAL CHOPS WITH MUSHROOMS AND WINE

2 tablespoons butter
2 rib or loin veal chops, 1 inch thick
½ cup sliced mushrooms
½ cup Marsala wine

Melt butter in a large skillet over medium low heat; add veal chops and sauté gently 15 to 20 minutes on each side. Transfer chops to a heated platter. Pour off all but 2 tablespoons of fat; add mushrooms and sauté until tender. Transfer mushrooms to chops. Add wine to pan, raise heat, and allow to thicken slightly. Pour over chops and serve. **Serves 2.**

VEAL PARMESAN

¾ pound veal scallops, cut ⅜ inch thick and pounded to ¼-inch thickness
1 tablespoon olive oil
¼ pound prosciutto, sliced thin
½ cup grated mozzarella cheese
1 8-ounce jar meatless spaghetti sauce

Preheat oven to 350° F. Heat oil in a medium skillet; add veal scallops, a few at a time, and sauté 2 minutes on each side. Transfer to a shallow baking dish and top each scallop with slices of prosciutto. Pour spaghetti sauce over scallops and top with grated cheese. Bake 25 minutes, or until sauce is bubbly and cheese has melted. **Serves 2.**

CABBAGE WITH PORK SAUSAGE

2 tablespoons butter
1 small onion, thinly sliced
$^{1}/_{2}$ cup coarsely shredded white cabbage
2 teaspoons red wine vinegar
2 sweet or hot Italian sausage, casings removed

Melt butter in a medium skillet; add onion and sauté over moderate heat until translucent. Add cabbage and stir, making sure that cabbage is coated with butter. Cook over moderate heat until cabbage begins to brown. Add vinegar and sausages; cover pan, reduce heat, and simmer about 45 minutes. **Serves 1.**

HAM STEAK

1   tablespoon butter
1/4   teaspoon instant coffee
1   8-ounce ham steak, cut 1/2 inch thick
1   small onion, thinly sliced
1/4   cup sour cream

Over moderate heat, melt butter in a 7-inch skillet; add instant coffee and stir until combined. Add ham steak and sauté until lightly browned. Remove ham steak to a warm plate. Add onions to skillet and sauté until lightly browned. Stir in sour cream; heat through and pour over ham steak. **Serves 1.**

SAUSAGE AND PEPPER FRITTATA

Try topping the frittata with some shredded mozzarella or Fontina cheese just before placing under the broiler.

1   small hot or sweet Italian sausage,
    casing removed
3   eggs
2   tablespoons grated Parmesan cheese
1/2   sweet green or red pepper, cut into
    1-inch julienne strips
1   tablespoon olive oil

Preheat oven to broil. In a small skillet, fry sausage over medium heat until brown and crumbly. Drain on absorbent paper. Beat eggs lightly; stir in cheese, sausage, and peppers. In a heavy, ovenproof 7-inch skillet, heat oil over medium heat until very hot. Add egg mixture and lower heat. Gently stir egg mixture with a wooden spoon and cook 2 to 3 minutes. Eggs should be firm but moist. **Serves 1.**

GLAZED RIBS

2 **pounds spareribs**
Salt
1 **large clove garlic, crushed**
¹/₃ **cup orange marmalade**
1 **tablespoon Dijon mustard**

Preheat oven to 350° F. Rub ribs thoroughly with salt and garlic. Place in a shallow baking pan and bake 45 minutes, turning occasionally. Meanwhile, melt marmalade in a small saucepan; add mustard and blend thoroughly. Remove ribs from oven and pour just enough marmalade over ribs to cover. Return pan to oven and continue cooking ribs another 15 minutes, basting frequently with remaining marmalade. **Serves 2.**

CAJUN CHICKEN WINGS

1   pound chicken wings
1   cup milk
1   teaspoon Tabasco sauce
Seasoned bread crumbs
Oil for deep frying

In a large bowl, combine chicken, milk, and Tabasco sauce. Marinate in refrigerator 1 hour. Drain wings and roll in bread crumbs; refrigerate 20 minutes. Heat oil to 375° F; fry chicken wings, a few at a time, about 12 minutes, or until crisp on the outside and cooked on the inside. **Serves 2.**

CURRIED CHICKEN QUARTERS

$\frac{1}{2}$ cup seasoned flour
$\frac{1}{2}$ cup peanut oil
1   tablespoon curry powder, or to taste
1   broiler-fryer chicken (about 2½ pounds), quartered, rinsed, and dried

Preheat oven to 375° F. Mix flour, oil, and curry powder together in a small bowl. Brush mixture evenly over chicken. Arrange chicken in a shallow pan and bake until juices run clear when thigh is pierced with a fork. **Serves 2.**

STUFFED CHICKEN BREASTS

2   whole chicken breasts, skinned, boned, and halved
2   slices Swiss cheese, cut ¼ inch thick
1   egg, beaten
Seasoned bread crumbs
Oil for deep frying

Pound chicken breasts to ⅛-inch thickness. Place a slice of cheese on each breast half and roll up; secure with toothpicks. Dip chicken rolls in egg, then roll in bread crumbs to coat. Allow to dry in refrigerator 1 hour. Heat oil to 375° F. Fry chicken rolls until golden, 12 to 15 minutes. **Serves 2.**

OVEN-FRIED FISH

¼   cup salad oil
¼   cup milk
1   egg, lightly beaten
1   pound fish fillets, such as perch, flounder, sole
½   cup cornflake or saltine cracker crumbs

Preheat oven to 475° F. Pour salad oil in a shallow baking dish and place in oven. Heat until oil is sizzling. Stir milk and egg together in a medium bowl. Dip fish fillets in milk-egg mixture, then roll in crumbs to coat. Arrange fillets on heated pan, return to oven, and bake 15 minutes, turning once. **Serves 2.**

ZUCCHINI BROIL

2   medium zucchini, washed, ends trimmed, and split in half lengthwise
1   tablespoon mayonnaise
1   tablespoon seasoned dry bread crumbs
1   tablespoon grated Parmesan cheese

Preheat oven to broil. Brush cut side of zucchini with mayonnaise. Sprinkle dry bread crumbs and Parmesan on top, coating evenly. Set zucchini, crumb side up, on a baking sheet and place under broiler about 6 inches from heat. Broil until crumbs are golden and zucchini is tender. Serve hot. **Serves 2.**

LINGUINE WITH PEPPERS

Pass the Parmesan cheese . . .

> **Olive oil**
> 1 **small clove garlic, crushed**
> 1 **small sweet red pepper, stem, seeds, and ribs removed, and cut into 1½-inch strips.**
> 4 **ounces linguine, cooked**
> **Parmesan cheese**

In a small skillet, heat 1 tablespoon oil; add garlic and peppers and cook over moderate heat until peppers are tender but still crisp. Remove from heat and discard garlic. Add linguine to pan and toss well, adding more oil if desired. Serve hot, topped with grated Parmesan cheese. **Serves 1.**

COTTAGE CHEESE PANCAKES

$\frac{1}{2}$ cup cottage cheese
2 eggs, lightly beaten
2 tablespoons all-purpose flour
$\frac{1}{8}$ teaspoon salt
$\frac{1}{8}$ teaspoon cinnamon, optional

In a medium bowl, mash cottage cheese until almost smooth; add eggs, flour, and salt. Mix well. Drop $\frac{1}{4}$ cup batter onto lightly greased hot griddle or heavy skillet. When bubbles appear on top, flip over and brown lightly on other side. **Serves 2.**

SOUFFLÉ FOR TWO

$\frac{1}{2}$ cup seasoned croutons
1 cup grated cheese
$1\frac{1}{2}$ cups milk
3 eggs, beaten
Freshly ground pepper

Preheat oven to 350° F. Place croutons in bottom of a greased 4-cup soufflé dish; sprinkle cheese on top. Mix together eggs, milk, and pepper; pour into dish and bake 1 hour. Serve immediately.

DESSERTS

APPLESAUCE

2 pounds cooking apples, peeled,
  seeded, and quartered
$^1/_2$ cup sugar
$^1/_2$ teaspoon cinnamon
1 teaspoon lemon juice
$^1/_8$ teaspoon nutmeg

In a medium saucepan, bring $^1/_2$ cup water to a boil; add apples and return water to boiling. Reduce heat; cover and simmer 20 to 25 minutes, stirring occasionally and adding more water if necessary. Add remaining ingredients, stirring until combined. Serve warm or cold. **Makes 3 cups.**

BAKED BANANAS FLAMBÉ

$1^1/_2$ tablespoons butter
2 large ripe bananas, peeled
1 tablespoon sugar
2 tablespoons rum, warmed

Preheat oven to 450° F. In a small baking or gratin dish, melt butter in oven. Remove dish from oven; roll bananas in melted butter and sprinkle with sugar. Return bananas to oven and bake 10 minutes or until tender. Remove from oven and pour warmed rum over bananas. Ignite. **Serves 2.**

FROZEN BANANAS AND CREAM

¹/₂ **cup heavy cream, whipped**
1   **small very ripe banana, mashed**
2   **tablespoons Irish cream liqueur**
¹/₄ **teaspoon ground ginger, optional**

Combine all ingredients in a small bowl; freeze at least 1 hour. **Serves 1.**

LINDT CHOCOLATE MOUSSE

This recipe serves 4, but no one has ever turned down seconds!

6 ounces Lindt chocolate, broken into pieces
1 cup heavy cream
1 egg
1 teaspoon sugar
Pinch cinnamon

In top of a double boiler, melt chocolate. Remove from heat; add cream, egg, and sugar and beat vigorously with a wire whisk until smooth. Refrigerate at least 3 hours. Beat again with a wire whisk until mixture is slightly thickened and fluffy. Pour into serving glasses, sprinkle with cinnamon, and chill again before serving. **Serves 2 to 4.**

EGGNOG

2 eggs
1 large banana, very ripe
1¹/₂ cups cold milk
¹/₂ cup Irish cream liqueur

Puree all ingredients in work bowl of food processor or blender. **Serves 2.**

That Extra Something

Though there are cooks and chefs who will maintain that great cooks are born, not made, we believe that the ability to be a good cook is really just a question of practice. In this chapter, we hope to provide a few hints that we've come across in the course of our cooking careers that may prove useful to you in the way of short-cuts, useful information, miscellaneous recipes, and little tidbits about the preparation of food that if your mother never told you, you probably never heard.

COOKING TIPS

- Flavored butters are an excellent way to cheer up an otherwise drab meal. Serve over vegetables, toast, or cooked pasta for some interesting variations.

SESAME BUTTER

¹/₂ cup butter
¹/₄ cup toasted sesame seeds

Melt the butter over low heat; add seeds and sauté until golden. Serve over vegetables.

EASY GARLIC BUTTER

2 cloves garlic, pressed
¹/₂ cup butter, at room temperature
3 tablespoons Parmesan cheese, optional

The secret to great garlic butter is to allow the butter and garlic mixture to stand for at least 30 minutes before serving. Blend garlic and butter thoroughly; add cheese and blend. Spread over vegetables, bread, or pasta, and top with cheese if desired.

HERB BUTTER

½   cup butter, softened

Any combination of the following:
1   tablespoon chopped fresh tarragon
1   tablespoon chopped fresh parsley
1   tablespoon chopped fresh oregano
1   tablespoon chopped fresh chives
1   tablespoon chopped fresh savory

Combine butter and herbs thoroughly. Serve over vegatables, spread on sandwiches, or melt and pour over pasta.

● Leftover meats such as beef and veal don't have to be drab. Slice the meat thin, brush with Dijon mustard, and roll in bread crumbs. Sauté in melted butter until golden. No one will know they're having leftovers!

● Cold summer soups look extra beautiful when served in large green or red pepper shells.

- A great substitute for breading: roll chicken or veal cutlets in ground almonds. Sauté in lots of butter and serve with pan juices and butter poured over.

- Perfect gravy. Actually, there is more than one way to make perfect pan gravy, but one good method is to blend the flour or cornstarch with beer before adding to pan juices. Not only does this add flavor but the carbonation in the beer disperses the flour evenly for a great-tasting, lumpless result.

- Also remember to substitute beer for cooking liquid the next time you braise or boil beef. The beer acts as a tenderizer for cheaper cuts of meats, and it adds a great flavor.

- Another gravy-making method is to substitute a tablespoon of packaged baking mix for the usual flour or cornstarch thickener. The baking mix can be added directly to pan juices and dissolves much more easily than plain flour.

- Concerned about calories? Use cornstarch as a thickener wherever possible in your cooking. Though cornstarch and flour have about the same amount of calories, you use about half as much cornstarch, and so save half the calories.

- Fresh mushrooms keep longer if stored in a brown paper bag in the vegetable bin than if stored in plastic.

- One cup of dried beans equals 2½ cups cooked beans.

- One cup of uncooked rice equals 3 cups cooked rice.

• Bel Paese or Gruyère cheese can be substituted for hard-to-find Italian Fontina.

• Grating cheese? Half a pound of cheese will yield approximately 2 cups grated cheese.

• The next time you have an outdoor barbecue, add ¼ cup cracked ice to each pound of hamburger before shaping into patties. A plumper, juicier result.

• For perfect hard-cooked eggs, with no touches of green around the yolks, place eggs in a saucepan with water to cover and 1 tablespoon salt. Bring to a hard boil over medium heat; immediately remove pan from heat and let sit 20 minutes. Immediately place eggs under cold water 2 to 3 minutes.

• Save leftover broccoli stalks; then slice and stir fry with other vegetables for a Chinese touch.

• When separating eggs, remove unwanted bits of yolks from white with the corner of a moistened tea towel.

• When making several omelettes, beat eggs and seasonings together in a bowl and use a ladle or measuring cup to pour out the right amount. Two large eggs measure about ⅓ cup; 3 eggs, ½ cup.

• To prevent butter from burning too quickly when sautéing, heat butter with oil in a ratio of 2 tablespoons of butter to 1 tablespoon oil. The oil allows the butter to reach a higher temperature without burning.

• When making a sauce, add only hot liquid to a hot roux.

BAKING TIPS

- Don't throw out Mom's old cookie sheet. Dark or dull baking pans absorb heat much faster and more evenly than do new, shiny baking pans. Shiny pans reflect heat, and so slow cooking time.

- To make your own superfine sugar, pour a small amount of granulated sugar into an electric coffee grinder. Turn the motor off and on a few times and, presto!, superfine sugar.

- If you have a gas stove, the proverbial "warm place" called for in many recipes might be right over your pilot light. Set bowls and containers on a trivet over light, and the resulting temperature should be just right for bread rising and the like.

- To determine when dough has doubled in bulk, lightly press tips of two fingers into dough; if dent remains, dough has doubled.

- A well-browned crust is easier to obtain if you use a dark bread pan rather than a shiny metal one.

- When making bread, fill a heatproof bowl with boiling water after bread has been turned out to be kneaded. When kneading is completed, pour out water. The bowl will be easy to wipe clean and warm as well, and the warmed bowl will help the yeast rise when dough is returned to it.

- Keep flour in one of the shakers used for confectioners' sugar, and use whenever small amounts of flour are called for in gravies, sauces, or for flouring pans and work surfaces.

• Though butter and margarine are interchangeable in most recipes, try to use butter for baking cookies and cakes. Real butter improves both flavor and keeping quality, and the butterfat tenderizes flour for an all-around better texture in baked goods.

• To prevent fruit pies from bubbling over, cut steam vents in crust.

• Store raisins or currants in a covered jar filled with brandy or apricot liqueur. Add to fruitcakes or breads when you want extra flavor.

• For never-fail pie pastry, add just a touch of vinegar (about a teaspoon) to insure a flaky, rich-tasting result.

• Add 1 teaspoon white corn syrup the next time you whip 1 cup cream (not ultra-pasteurized cream). The syrup will stabilize the cream, keep it from separating, and it will stay fresh for days. A much better result than unflavored-gelatin methods, and a whole lot easier!

• Why spend money on chocolate chips? A much better method is to purchase good quality, bulk chocolate and chip it yourself. Store in a covered container, preferably in the refrigerator. You get higher quality and a better tasting result.

CHIPPED CHOCOLATE FUDGE

12 ounces chocolate, broken into chips (a
semisweet or Lindt chocolate is best)

1 14-ounce can sweetened condensed
milk

2 teaspoons vanilla extract

$^1/_2$ cup chopped walnuts or pecans

In the top of a double boiler, melt together chocolate
and milk. Remove from heat; allow to cool slightly and
add vanilla. Beat at medium speed of electric mixer until
the mixture loses some of its gloss and thickens slightly.
Pour into a well-buttered 8-inch square pan and top with
nuts, pressing them down gently. Cut into squares while
still warm. **Makes about 2 pounds.**

• Speaking of chocolate, the following recipe makes
the best hot fudge sauce we've ever tasted.

BEST HOT FUDGE SAUCE

$^3/_4$ cup heavy cream

4 tablespoons butter

$^1/_2$ cup sugar

$^1/_2$ cup brown sugar, firmly packed

$^2/_3$ cup unsweetened cocoa

In the top of a double boiler, heat cream, butter, and sugars together until sugar is dissolved and butter is melted. Add cocoa all at once and stir until well blended. To serve, reheat over hot water. **Makes about 2 cups.**

• To make gorgeous chocolate curls for decorating cakes and tortes, all you need is a piece of chocolate and a swivel-bladed vegetable parer. Chocolate should be about 4 inches by $1^{3}/_{4}$ inches. Allow chocolate to stand in a warm place for 15 minutes, or until chocolate can be cut without crumbling. When ready, place chocolate flat side up in the palm of your hand and move vegetable parer toward you lengthwise along chocolate, pressing firmly. Place chocolate curls on a plate and chill until hard, about 20 minutes.

• To make your own sweetened condensed milk, combine 1 cup instant nonfat dry milk with $1/_3$ cup boiling water. Add $2/_3$ cup confectioners' sugar and 3 tablespoons butter. Transfer to work bowl of food processor or blender and process until thick. Makes about $1^{1}/_{4}$ cups. Store, covered, in refrigerator, for up to one month.

TIME-SAVERS AND OTHER USEFUL INFORMATION

• Freeze leftovers in individual tinfoil or ovenproof containers. Cover with foil, label, and store in sealable bags in freezer. Most homemade TV dinners can be cooked at 400° F about 50 minutes.

• Place aluminum foil underneath the napkin in your bread basket to help warmed rolls and breads keep their heat longer when brought to the table.

• Here's a restaurant trick to help keep finely chopped parsley from clumping. Wrap chopped parsley in a kitchen towel or a triple layer of cheesecloth. Hold under cold running water, squeezing out liquid until water runs pale green. Squeeze out excess water again. Parsley may be used immediately, or refrigerated in an airtight container up to 5 days.

• Add 1 tablespoon of kirsch, Cointreau, or brandy to 1 cup fruit preserves or jam. This makes a delicious topping for pancakes or crêpes.

• When serving sliced fresh fruit at a buffet or luncheon, top apple slices with a little lemon juice. Not only does this prevent discoloration but it adds a subtle, almost perfumed quality to the apples that's delicious!

⌒ Index ⌒